THE BEST
MODERN
PIANO
BOOK
FOR BEGINNERS

1 2 3 4 5 6 7

How this Series Works

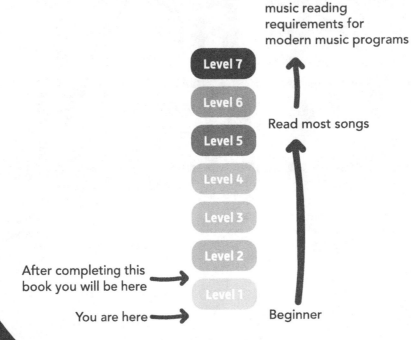

Beat the college-level music reading requirements for modern music programs

Level 7

Level 6

Level 5

Level 4

Level 3

Level 2

After completing this book you will be here →

Level 1

You are here →

Read most songs

Beginner

After completing this book you will be able to study, read, and play any song in these levels:

Level 1: Notation

Level 1: Leadsheet

Find your favorite songs at bestsheetmusic.com

First Edition 2021

ISBN: 978-1-7365547-6-0
ISBN: (Kindle): 978-1-7365547-6-0

@xz
www.bestmusiccoach.com
facebook.com/bestmusiccoach
youtube.com/bestmusiccoach
twitter.com/bestmusiccoach
instagram.com/bestmusiccoach

Book Design by Adam Hay Studio
Diagrams and Illustrations by Arron Leishman
Developmental Edit by Link Harnsberger
Copy Edit by Michael Britton

Welcome to Best Music Coach!

A note to adult students and parents

I am thrilled that you chose this book and our coaches to guide you, or your family, on your musical journey. We are here to answer all your musical questions and to empower our students, readers, and coaches to discover and achieve their musical goals. We also provide students with a clear path towards their musical potential and goals with fully customizable and inclusive learning experiences paired with effective teaching methods.

Many students begin playing the piano only to become disillusioned with the books they are using the learn. The goal of this book is to get you, the student, to play your favorite songs and keep the fun of learning music and to make it more simple, easy to follow, and clear to ensure the best musical education. This book, and the whole series, is designed to take you from zero (or close to zero if you have already begun to play) to music-reading, piano-playing hero! The ultimate goal is to give you the freedom to play any song in any genre. This means playing anything from Beethoven to The Beatles, Boys II Men to The Beach Boys.

For best results with this book, work with a qualified piano coach in weekly sessions of 30 minutes (ages 5—10) or 60 minutes (ages 11—adult).

Good luck, keep those fingers warm, and I wish you many hours of happy practicing and playing.

Dan Spencer - Lead Coach

**I am here for you.
Get free lessons and community
facebook.com/groups/musicmakersofficial**

Contents

1

2

3

Open QR code?

1. On an iPhone open the camera. On Android, download and open a QR code scanner application.

2. Hold your phone so you can see the QR code on the screen, and the screen is in focus.

3. On iPhones, tap the banner that asks you if you want to open the QR code. On Android, tap the button that asks you to open the QR code.

Want 80,000+ songs to play + a free music theory course? Check out this offer now. Click the link or scan the QR code. https://music.bestmusiccoach.com/piano-next-steps

How This Book Works

FREE Audio and Video Examples

This book comes with video examples of exercises and songs as well as a 30 day practice journal and your first 10 songs. Any time you see the icon (23) it is showing the video example number for you to listen to or watch to help you understand the song or exercise. All video examples, 30 day practice journal, and your first 10 songs can be found by scanning the QR code below with your device or at

bestmusiccoach.com/books

1. Click on "Piano."

2. Click on "Free Examples."

3. Create a free account and get started—click "Login to Enroll."

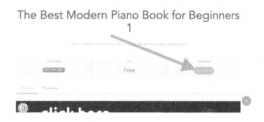

Do This With Your Coach:

Any time you see the "Coach" symbol below, I recommend taking this next step with a music teacher to avoid undesireable results, because using **any** book for this step is not optimal.

Song Titles and Writers

Many songs are titled and the songwriters who originally wrote the songs are credited in this book. You will see the following format before songs, but not exercises.

Song Title

Songwriter/Composer

Songs credited to "Best Music Coach" are by the author.

What You Will Need

A piano or keyboard!

You will need an acoustic or electric piano or keyboard with all keys in good working order. Get your keyboard/piano fixed if

- Any keys stick
- Any keys are harder to press down than the others
- Any keys do not make sound

How to Buy a Piano or Keyboard

If you intend on purchasing a keyboard or piano here are our recommendations

4. Buy your piano/keyboard from a reputable retailer and brand.

5. Check reviews of the piano/keyboard on multiple websites.

6. Try out the piano/keyboard in the store.

7. Make sure you have enough space at home to fit the piano/keyboard. Measure with a tape measure to ensure a good fit!

8. Electric keyboards: buy a keyboard with 88 keys if possible

9. Electric keyboards: buy a keyboard with weighted keys or "acoustic action". This will mimic the way the keys of an acoustic piano respond to touch. It makes for a more enjoyable and controlled playing experience.

10. Electric keyboards: buy a keyboard with velocity sensitivity. This will allow you to control how loud and quiet you play.

11. Electric keyboards: a height adjustable keyboard stand.

12. Buy a hight-adjustable piano stool, this will make all the difference in the world when it is time to play.

Read more about buying a piano and which ones we recommend at bestmusiccoach.com/blog

Your First Lesson

Everything you will learn and need to know in your first lesson!

What Am I?

As soon as you play a piano or keyboard, you become three things:

1. A piano/keyboard player

2. A musician

3. An artist

Piano/Keyboard Player

There is no better option between an acoustic piano and a keyboard (more on the differences between the two later). It is not "cheating" or "wrong" to play a keyboard or a piano. They both have different professional applications, but you will find that for now, you will be set up for success with either one, regardless of your goals for music in the future.

Musician

As a musician, you develop musical skills and talents that are transferable to any and all instruments and musical disciplines. For example, if you memorize a song on the piano, you will be able to play some version of it relatively quickly on a guitar. The study and development of basic musical skills is called musicianship.

Artist

The word "artist" makes many people think of a painter, or sculptor. They are right, both painting and sculpture are forms of art. The term "artist" can also be applied to writers, chefs, designers, architects, baristas, and many other professions. Music is a type of art, and musicians are artists.

Original Artist

When you create new music or sounds, you are an original artist. This can be as simple as playing one note of your piano, or as complex as writing a twenty-minute free-jazz, fusion, prog-rock odyssey.

Interpretive Artist

If you are playing music someone else has written, you might think of yourself as an interpretive artist. You are taking someone else's idea and using your creativity and artistry to add to it, change it, or shape it differently in some way. Neither type of artist is better than the other: they are two different ways of approaching music. You can be original, interpretive, or both!

Recommended Listening

Listening to music is like jet fuel for making progress as a musician. Listen to these artists as much as you can. Listen to their studio albums, compositions, and live performances of their work.

Gregg Allman
Johann Sebastian Bach
Count Basie
Jon Batiste
Ludwig van Beethoven
Dave Brubeck
David Bryan
Ray Charles
Frédéric Chopin
Chick Corea
Claude Debussy
George Duke
Brian Eno
Bill Evans
Ben Folds
Erroll Garner
Robert Glasper
Herbie Hancock
Earl Hines

Ahmad Jamal
Keith Jarrett
Billy Joel
Elton John
Booker T. Jones
Scott Joplin
Lang Lang
Jerry Lee Lewis
Franz Liszt
Jon Lord
Ray Manzarek
Les McCann
Brad Mehldau
Freddie Mercury
Thelonius Monk
Jelly Roll Morton
Wolfgang Amadeus Mozart
Oscar Peterson

Bud Powell
Billy Preston
Sergei Rachmaninoff
Little Richard
Sviatoslav Richter
Arthur Rubinstein
Jordan Rudess
Leon Russell
Clara Schumann
Robert Schumann
Horace Silver
Hiromi Uehara
Billy Strayhorn
Art Tatum
Jean-Yves Thibaudet
McCoy Tyner
Fats Waller
Stevie Wonder
Richard Wright

It might be fun (and also a good exercise to improve your playing) to make a video diary of yourself playing piano every day or every week to track your progress over time. If you decide to do this and post your videos to YouTube, Facebook, TikTok, Instagram, or any social media, tag @bestmusiccoach for reshares, encouragement, and free tips and advice!

Want 80,000+ songs to play + a free music theory course? Check out this offer now. Click the link or scan the QR code. https://music.bestmusiccoach.com/piano-next-steps

The Different Types of Pianos and Keyboards

Acoustic Pianos

Acoustic keyboards make sound without the use of electricity.

Grand Piano

Can range in size from 4 to 9 feet in length.

Makes sound when internal hammers hit strings.

Upright Piano

Smaller than a grand piano, with a different sound.

Makes sound when internal hammers hit strings.

Harmonium

Small and compact.

Makes sound by pumping air over metal reeds.

Harpsichord

Less common than pianos.

Makes sound when strings are plucked mechanically

Melodica

Small, portable.

Makes sound when air is blown through it.

Electric Pianos

Electric keyboards use electricity to make sound.

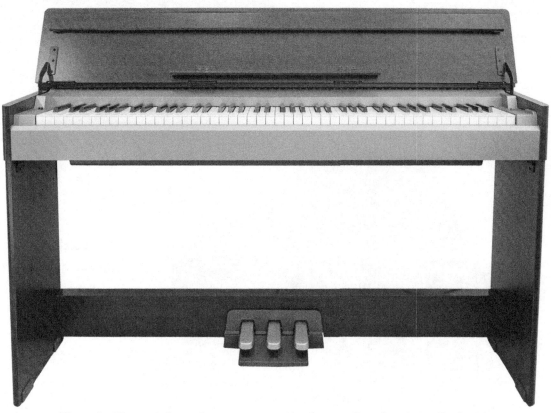

Electric Piano (above)

There are typically 3 to10 pre-programmed "voices", which sound like different types of pianos, as well as a harpsichord.

Analogue Synthesizer (below)

Manipulates the sound the synthesizer makes by combining and modifying different electric sounds.

Digital Synthesizer

Digital synthesizers with speakers generate sound. Others require amplification.

You can manipulate the sounds the synthesizer makes by modifying and changing the different "voices".

Digital synthesizers can sound like many different instruments.

Digital synthesizers can double as MIDI controllers.

Digital Synthesizer with speakers

Digital Synthesizer without speakers

MIDI Controller

Uses digital signals to create sound through a computer.

MIDI controllers do not make sound on their own.

Parts of Your Piano

1 Keyboard

Where you will place your fingers to play the piano! There are 88 keys on the keyboard.

2 Housing

The housing can look different on different pianos. It surrounds the piano like a candy wrapper.

3 Lid

Opening and closing the lid changes the sound and volume of the piano.
Open Lid: Louder, more resonant.
Closed Lid: Quieter, less resonant.

4 Strings

While there are 88 Keys, there can be up to 230 strings! Some keys in the middle and right side of the keyboard strike as many as three strings at the same time. Each string in the groups of three sound the same, this helps the piano sound louder a more full sound.

5 Hammers

When you press a key on the keyboard it moves a hammer which strikes a string, which is how the piano makes sound. In the picture, you can see hammers rising up to strike strings, as well as hammers that are in their resting position.

5a Raised hammers quickly strike the strings to make a sound.

5b Lowered hammers are waiting to be played!

6 Dampers

Dampers rest on the string until the moment before the hammer strikes the strings. The damper returns to rest on the strings to silence the sound of the piano.

6a Raised dampers allow the strings to make sound.

6b Lowered dampers stop the strings from making sound.

7 Tuning Pins

The strings attach to tuning pins. These pins can be turned with tools to increase or decrease the tension on the strings, which changes the sound of the string to a lower or higher sound. This allows a person who is a professional piano tuner to tune a piano.

8 Soundboard

Made from wood, the soundboard lies under the strings and reflects and amplifies the sound of the strings.

9 The Plate or Harp

The plate is made from metal and holds the strings in place.

Parts of Your Keyboard

1 **Keyboard**

Where you will place your fingers to play the piano! There are 88 keys on the keyboard.

2 **Housing**

The housing can look different on different keyboards. It surrounds the keyboard like a candy wrapper.

3 **Modulation and Pitchbend Wheels**

These wheels will change the sound of the synthesizer or keyboard in different ways.

Modulation wheel: Increases the amount of any effects on the synth sound.

Pitch bend: makes the note, or notes being played change to a higher or lower pitch.

4 **Tone, Volume, Effects, Pads, Patch Controls**

Each keyboard has a different layout of these controls. Read through the user manual for your keyboard to learn more about your instrument and how to use these knobs, sliders, pads, and buttons. Ask your coach for help with understanding your instrument.

What is MIDI?

MIDI stands for Musical Instrument Digital Interface.

No audio or sound is sent from a MIDI controller. MIDI works as a digital signal, talking in the language of computers (binary) with 1s and 0s and sending it to a computer. These binary messages tell the computer

1. Which key you press.

2. The time when you press the key.

3. The time you release the key.

4. How hard you press the key. This is called "velocity" and will sometimes make a note sound louder the harder you press and quieter the softer you press.

5. If you change the pressure on the key (after-touch).

The computer understands and then responds to these 1s and 0s, making sound or recording the pattern of MIDI signals that the keyboard sends to it.

How Your Keyboard Makes Sound

1. Electricity powers the keyboard.

2. You press down on a key.

3. Through hardware and software systems, the keyboard

4. Generates a sound through built-in speakers.

5. Generates sound through external speakers.

6. Sends a MIDI signal to a computer. The computer makes a sound from the MIDI input.

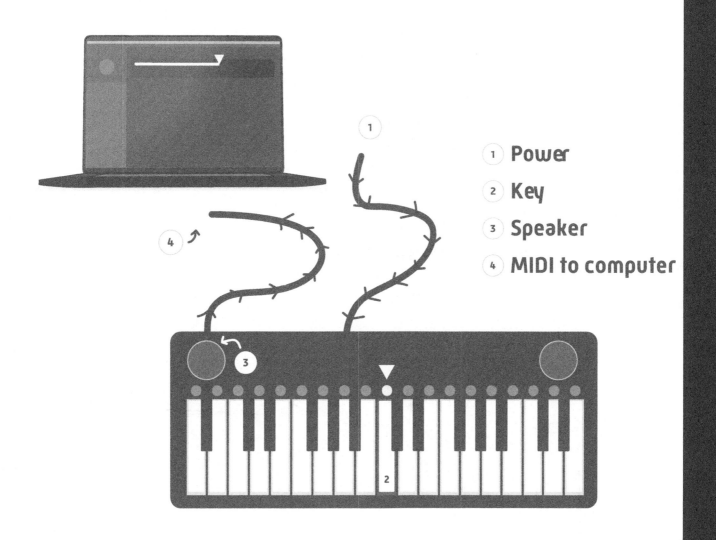

1. **Power**
2. **Key**
3. **Speaker**
4. **MIDI to computer**

How to Play the Piano

How to Sit at the Piano

1. Adjust the height of your piano bench so that your knees are just below the keyboard.

2. To sit the correct distance from the piano, make fists with your hands while keeping your back comfortably straight. Your fists should reach the end of the keys. Your fists should reach without you needing to lean forward or stretch your arms. We will call this a "Distance Check."

3. To sit in line with the center of the piano/keyboard, find the brand name in the middle of the keyboard. If there is no brand name, or it is off to the side, do your best to find the center of the keyboard and align it with your belly button.

4. Leave some space between your calves and the piano bench. You may need to move the piano bench back or forward to get a good placement.

5. Plant your feet firmly on the floor, or on a stool if your legs are not long enough to reach the floor.

6. Make sure your back is straight, but not rigid.

7. Keep your head in a neutral position over your body.

① Seated position

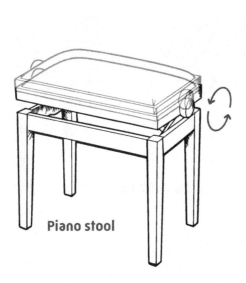

Piano stool

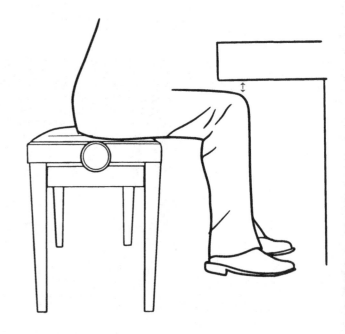

② Distance Check

③ Align

Brand name

Belly button

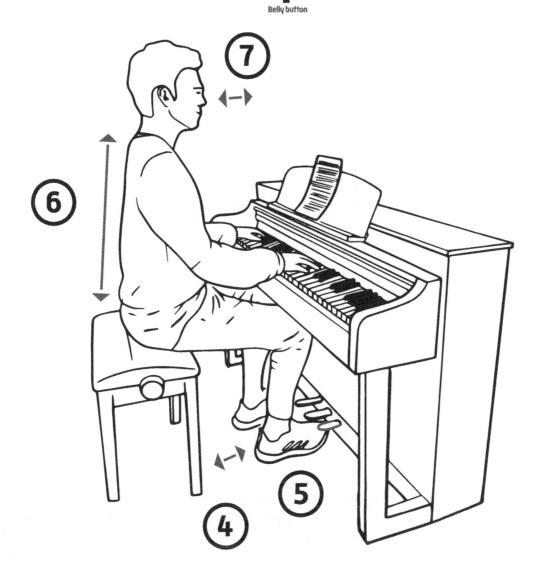

How to Place Your Hands on the Piano

Distance

Perform a Distance Check to make sure you are not too close or far away from the keyboard.

> ### Why is the Finger Curl Important?
> Keeping your fingers curled will:
>
> **1.** Help you play much faster than with flat fingers.
>
> **2.** Play the piano with less effort.
>
> **3.** Maintain more control over the keys as you press down and release them.

How to Curl Your Fingers

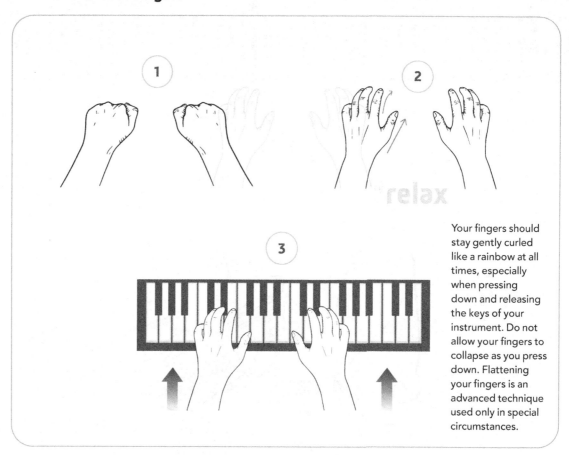

Your fingers should stay gently curled like a rainbow at all times, especially when pressing down and releasing the keys of your instrument. Do not allow your fingers to collapse as you press down. Flattening your fingers is an advanced technique used only in special circumstances.

Step 1   With your arms by your side, make fists with both hands and squeeze the fists tight.

Step 2   Relax your hands and look at the way your fingers curve and your thumb floats at an angle to your fingers.

Step 3   Bring your hands up and place them on the piano without changing the curl of the fingers.

> **How you play the piano is called "technique" (tek-neek). When you play the piano following the guidelines for "How to Sit at the Piano" and "How to Place your Hands on the Piano", it is called playing with "good" or "correct" technique.**

How to Understand the Keyboard

Low Sounds and High Sounds

To the left of the piano there are low sounds. As you play keys that are more to the right, they make higher sounds. From left to right, each key makes a higher sound than the key before it.

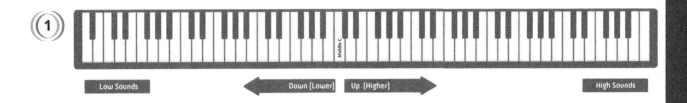

Patterns

The keyboard has some easy patterns to spot, we will use those patterns to help us understand where we are on the keyboard.

The Black Key Pattern

On the keyboard there is a distinct pattern of black keys.
We can spot black keys together in

    1. Groups of two

    2. Groups of three

The groups of two and three black keys are repeated the entire keyboard.

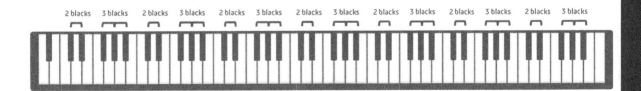

The 12-Key Pattern

12-Key Pattern Breakdown - Part 1

There is a pattern that repeats every 12 keys on the piano. We can make finding this pattern even easier by dividing the 12-key pattern into two parts.

Part 1 of the pattern is the three white keys that are around the group of two black keys. Counting the white and black keys in this section we have five keys. The white key all the way to the left of the group of two black keys (key 1) is the first key in the 12-key pattern.

12 Keys – Part 1

12-Key Pattern Breakdown - Part 2

Part 2 of the pattern is the four white keys that are around the group of three black keys. Counting the white and black keys of this section, we have seven keys. The white key all the way to the right of the group of three black keys (key 12) is the last key in the 12-key pattern.

12 Keys – Part 2

The Complete 12-Key Pattern

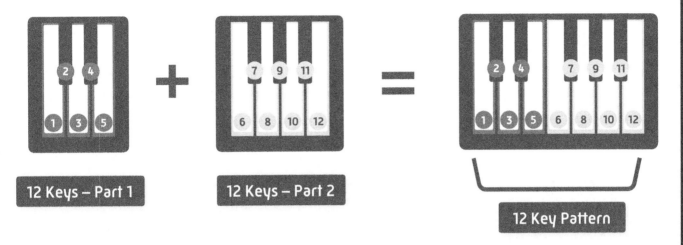

12 Keys – Part 1 + 12 Keys – Part 2 = 12 Key Pattern

How the Full 12-Key Pattern Repeats

The 12-key pattern repeats over and over again for the entire keyboard. Every time it repeats, it sounds higher than the last 12-key group when going from left to right.

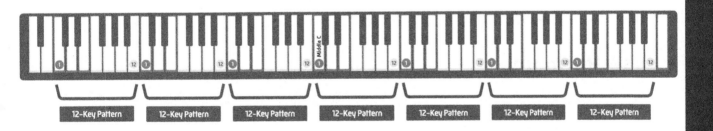

The Four Elements of Music

There are four fundamental elements that come together to create music.

(2) Rhythm

Rhythm is the foundation of music. It defines the passage of time through the presence and absence of sound. It is the most basic and fundamental component of any musical expression.

Clap your hands together slowly four times in a row. When you clap there is sound, when you are not clapping there is an absence of sound. This is rhythm.

(3) Pitch

In music we call most sounds pitches. A pitch is a single sound. Open your mouth and say "aaaah" just like you would at the doctor's or dentist's office. The sound you are making is a pitch, which you can sometimes call a note. A note is a way of measuring a pitch and giving it a name. More on that later!

(4) Melody

A melody is a series of sequential pitches that takes place over time. Many songwriters and composers try to make "pleasing" melodies. What you find pleasing may be different from what someone else thinks of as pleasing. Melody is subjective, which means that everyone can feel differently about a melody, and no one is right or wrong, they just have their opinions. In a melody, there is never more than one sound at a time. If you play several piano keys slowly, one at a time so that they sound individually, that is a melody.

(5) Harmony

Harmony is the combination of at least two different notes sounding together at the same time. These combination sounds are called chords. Play two piano keys at the same time to hear a chord.

> ## Tone
>
> Another word for tone is timbre (tim-ber). Tone is the color or quality of a sound; how you play a pitch or harmony. Your tone changes depending on several factors.
>
> - Piano body shape, type, materials, and size.
> - Keyboard settings.
> - How hard and how gently you press the keys when you play.

The Basic Musical Alphabet:

A B C D E F G

- The first seven letters of the regular alphabet.
- Repeats back to A after G.
- Ascends infinitely.
- Descends infinitely.
- Begin on any of the seven letters and count up or down the basic musical alphabet in ascending or descending order.
- These letters are note names, a way of giving names to pitches.

(6) The Basic Musical Alphabet: Circle

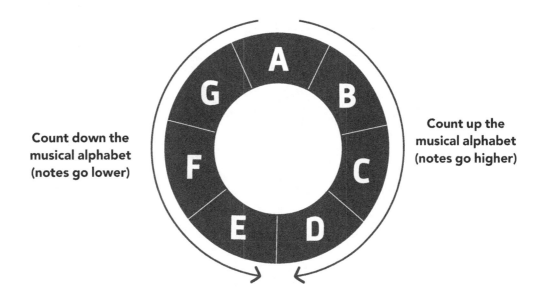

Count down the musical alphabet (notes go lower)

Count up the musical alphabet (notes go higher)

The Basic Musical Alphabet: Vertical

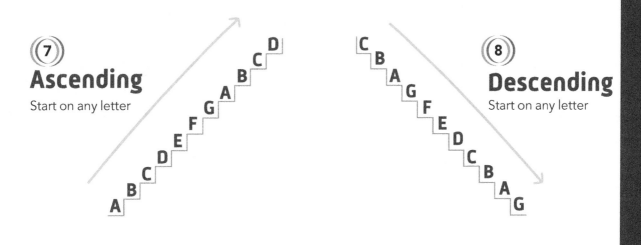

(7) Ascending
Start on any letter

(8) Descending
Start on any letter

How to Remember the Names of the White Keys

Reminder: There is a 12-key pattern that repeats over and over again on the keyboard of the piano.

How to Remember the White Keys: Step 1

- Start on the Letter C of the basic musical alphabet.
- C is the name of the first key in the 12-key pattern.
- It is called the C key because when you press it, it makes a C note.
- Just like the 12-key pattern repeats, the names of the white keys repeat with the 12-key pattern.

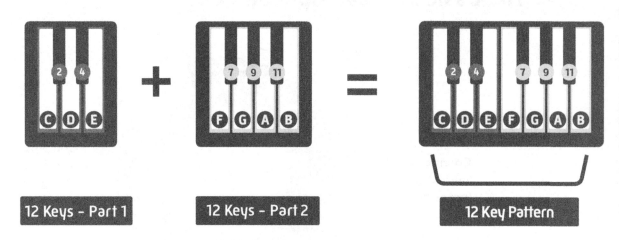

12 Keys - Part 1   **12 Keys - Part 2**   **12 Key Pattern**

Play It and Say It!

1. Start on any C note on the piano.
2. Play the C note with your dominant hand's index (pointer) finger.
3. Say "C" aloud.
4. Play the D note to the right of the C note and say "D" aloud.
5. Continue on for the entire piano with the E, F, G, A, and B notes.

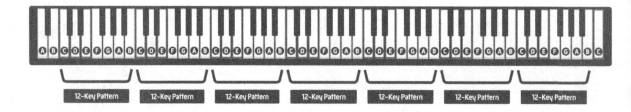

How to Remember the White Keys: Step 2

Low to High

Start by going from lowest to highest-sounding; left to right.

1. Find and play all the C keys on the piano.
2. Find and play all the D keys on the piano.
3. Find and play all the E keys on the piano.
4. Find and play all the F keys on the piano.
5. Find and play all the G keys on the piano.
6. Find and play all the A keys on the piano.
7. Find and play all the B keys on the piano.

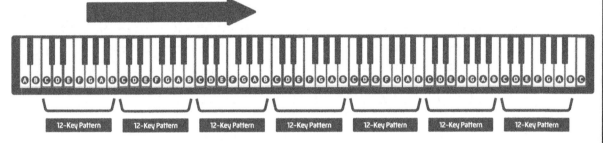

High to Low

When going the lowest to highest is easy, go from the highest to the lowest for each key.

8. Find and play all the C, D, E, F, G , A, and B keys on the piano.

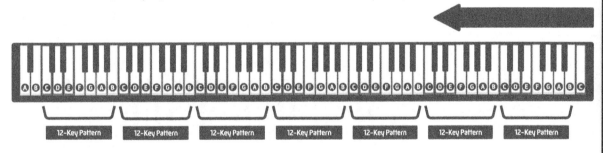

Middle C

What is Middle C?

Middle C, also known as C4, is the fourth C key from the left on an 88-key keyboard. Middle C is generally found near the name of the piano or keyboard maker. It is approximately the middle note of the instrument.

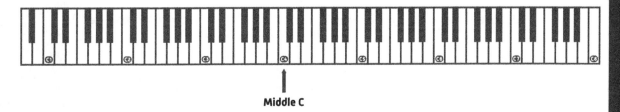

Middle C

⑨ How to Find Middle C

Middle C sounds the same on all keyboards. Depending on the number of keys on your keyboard, it can be found in different places.

1. Count your white and black keys carefully.
2. Take the number of white and black keys on your keyboard.
   Use that number to match up your keyboard with one of the six shown below.
3. Memorize the location of Middle C.

Middle C on an 88-Key Keyboard (The 24th White Key from the Left)

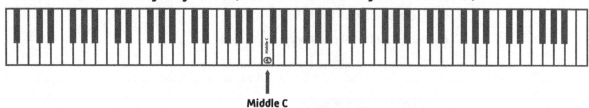

Middle C

Middle C on a 76-Key Keyboard (The 20th White Key from the Left)

Middle C

Middle C on a 61-Key Keyboard (The 15th White Key from the Left)

Middle C

Middle C on a 49-Key Keyboard (The 15th White Key from the Left)

Middle C

Middle C on a 32-Key Keyboard (The 12th White Key from the Left)

Middle C

Middle C on a 25-Key Keyboard (The 8th White Key from the Left)

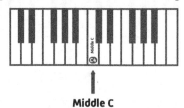

Middle C

Younger students and students who need a reminder can place a small, removable sticker on their Middle C to find it easily.

Finger Numbers

To help keep track of hands and fingers, and know which hands and fingers to use, we will assign numbers to each finger.

> **Finger Numbers**
>
> **1.** Both thumbs
>
> **2.** Both index fingers
>
> **3.** Both middle fingers
>
> **4.** Both ring fingers
>
> **5.** Both pinky fingers

Hand Abbreviations

- The right hand = RH
- The left hand = LH

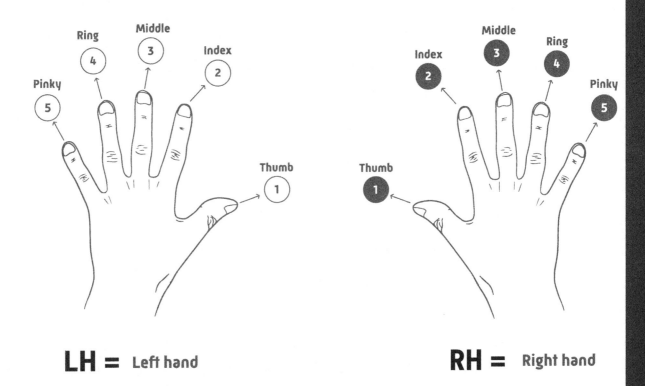

LH = Left hand

RH = Right hand

Finger Order

Finger order means which fingers are used to play different keys on the piano.

How to Read Piano Diagrams

Each song and exercise in this book has a small piano diagram above it that shows you three things.

> **1.** Which keys you will play in the song or exercise.
>
> **2.** Which hand and fingers you will use on the keys to play the music.
>
> **3.** Where Middle C is, so you can put your fingers on the correct keys.

Hands and Fingers

Left Hand Finger Numbers

Left hand finger numbers are black, with a white background.

Right Hand Finger Numbers

Right hand finger numbers are white, with a black background.

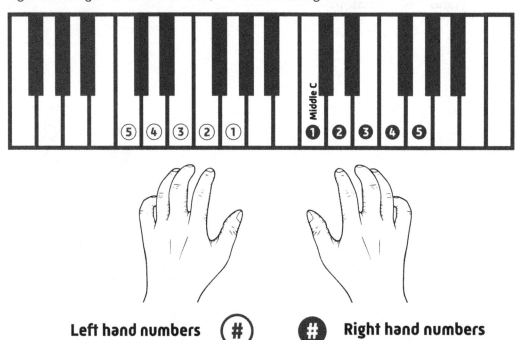

Left hand numbers (#) (#) **Right hand numbers**

Key Names

The names of the keys you will be playing are underneath the keys.

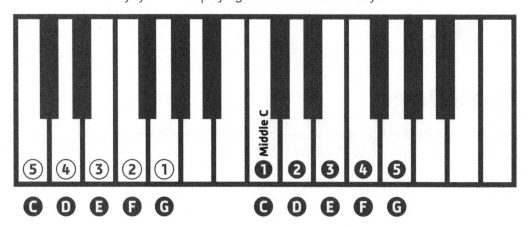

Review: Your First Lesson

If any of these review points are not clear, or you can't remember what they mean, go back to the page or pages and review. Move forward in the book only when you understand and can remember all of these review points!

- What Am I?

- Recommended Listening

- The Different Types of Pianos and Keyboards

- Parts of Your Piano

- How Your Piano Makes Sound

- Parts of Your Keyboard

- What is MIDI?

- How Your Keyboard Makes Sound

- How to Play the Piano
    How to Sit at the Piano
    How to Place Your Hands on the Piano

- How to Understand the Keyboard
    The Black Key Pattern
    The 12-Key Pattern

- The Four Elements of Music
    Rhythm
    Pitch
    Melody
    Harmony

- The Basic Musical Alphabet

- How to Remember the Names of the White Keys

- Middle C
    What is Middle C?
    How to Find Middle C
- Finger Numbers

- How to Read Piano Diagrams

How to Play Your First Full Song

This chapter holds all the information you will need to start playing songs!

Notes

Musicians play, read, and write rhythm with symbols called "notes." Each kind of note is written differently.

open notehead　　　　**open notehead**　　　　**closed notehead**

　　　　　　　　　　　　　　stem　　　　　　　　　　stem

> The different kinds of notes show how long or how short a sound should be. A note's duration is called "rhythmic value." A whole note has a larger rhythmic value than a quarter note.

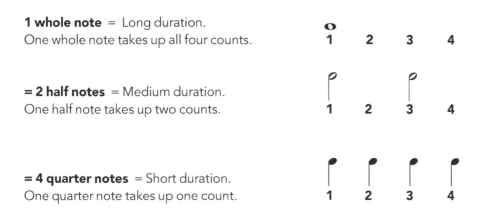

1 whole note = Long duration.
One whole note takes up all four counts.

= 2 half notes = Medium duration.
One half note takes up two counts.

= 4 quarter notes = Short duration.
One quarter note takes up one count.

The Staff

The staff has five, parallel lines. All the music you read for the rest of this book will take place on the staff.

Staff (five parallel lines)

> Two or more lines of staff are called "staves."
> Oftentimes a staff with music on it is called a "line" of music.

How to Play the Notes

Play the Notes: Right Hand Only

The keys of the piano correspond to the notes on the staff. As you read up the Basic Musical Alphabet, the notes are higher on the staff. As you read down, the notes are lower. The lowest notes that the right hand plays here are C and D, which are both below the staff. The box that shows you where to place your fingers is called a "key box."

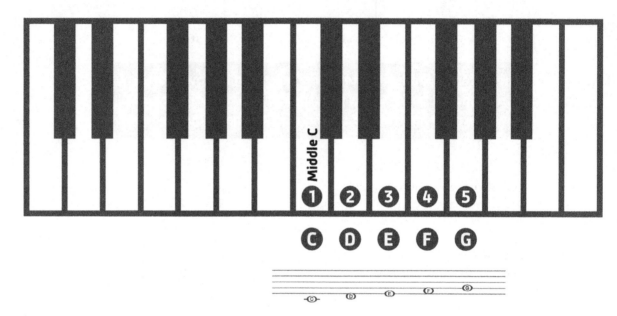

Extra Symbols: Press and hold key = ↑   Count = count the numbers aloud

Right Hand: Whole Notes

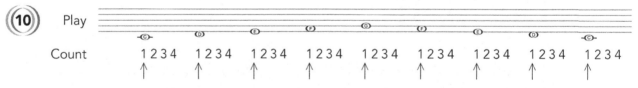

Right Hand: Half Notes

Right Hand: Quarter Notes

Play the Notes: Left Hand Only

The left hand starts on the C below (to the left of) Middle C. Remember the different C's on the piano? Middle C is C4, the C that the left hand plays with the 5th finger is C3. C3 sounds lower than C4. The notes for the left hand are in a different place on the staff when compared to the right hand notes. The C note for the left hand is on the staff, the C note for the right hand is below the staff.

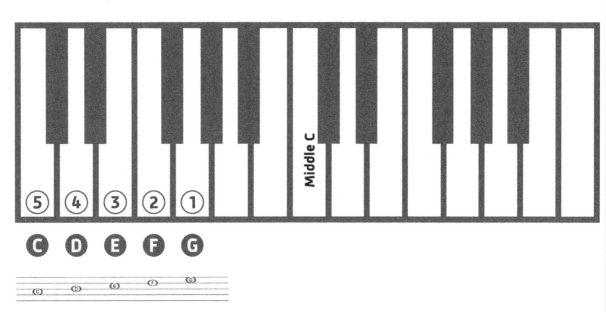

Left Hand: Whole Notes

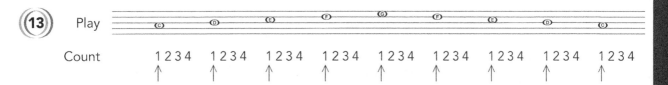

Left Hand: Half Notes

Left Hand: Quarter Notes

The Metronome

A metronome is a device or software application that produces a sound at even intervals of time that can be sped up or slowed down. Metronome speed is measured by how many times it makes a sound or "clicks" per minute. This is called "beats per minute" (BPM). Every click of the metronome is considered a "beat" for examples in this book.

The speed at which you should complete an example or group of examples will be shown like this: **120**
This means to set a metronome to 60 BPM and begin the click before you start the example.

Starting Out:

Sometimes taking on a new exercise at the recommended speed will be too hard at first. If this is the case go through the exercise carefully by

1. Count and clap the rhythm of the music without the metronome.

- Do your best to keep an even speed.

2. Set the metronome to a slower speed, clap and count the music.

- 50 BPM is a good starting point.
- Increase the metronome speed by 5 BPM when you are comfortable and are not making any mistakes.
- Continue increasing the speed of the metronome until you can clap the example at the suggested speed without making any mistakes.

3. Play the music with your instrument. First without the metronome, then use the metronome to slowly increase the speed of your playing, just like steps 1 and 2.

There are three main types of metronome:

Count In
What is a Count In?

So that all musicians know where the beat is in a song, and how fast the song is going to be, someone can "count in" the number of beats at the speed the song is going to be at one or two times before starting the song. Listen to the following examples to hear count ins.

LISTEN

I Saw Her Standing There	The Beatles
Patience	Guns N' Roses
Hey Ya	Outkast

Who Performs the Count In?

In a Group

In a group either the drummer, "band leader", conductor or music director will count the song in. Coaches will sometimes count in for you in lessons.

By Yourself

When you are playing or practicing by yourself you can give a count in with a metronome, or if you are not playing with a metronome, that as close to the desired metronome speed as possible. Start by performing count ins aloud, and soon you will perform count ins silently, in your head.

Count In: Application

You will give yourself a count in before playing the exercises and songs in this book.

(16) Count In: Four

- Listen carefully to the pulse from your metronome.
  When you feel you can anticipate the timing between the clicks:

- Count "1, 2, 3, 4" aloud with each number you speak happening at the same time as a click.

Be as precise as possible and speak exactly with the clicking sound, not before or after.

Count In Goal: Four Clicks then Count

- Listen to the click for as long as you need until you can anticipate the timing between clicks. Perform a count in. When this is easy and you can do it consistently:

- Listen to the click for 16 clicks. On the 17th click, perform a count in. When this is easy and you can do it consistently:

- Listen to the click for 8 clicks. On the 9th click, perform a count in. When this is easy and you can do it consistently:

- Listen to the click for 4 clicks. On the 5th click, perform a count in.

How to Clap Rhythms

You are encouraged to bounce, rock, sway, and move your body with the click of the metronome!

Reminder: You can start without the metronome or slow the metronome down if you need to. Give yourself a count in of "1, 2, 3, 4" along with the metronome before starting these exercises.

Key: Clap Hands = ↑   Count = count aloud

How to Clap Quarter Notes

1. Clap on every beat (on every click) of the metronome. These are called quarter notes.

2. Try to be precise as possible and clap exactly with the clicking sound, not before or after.

3. When this is comfortable, repeat "1, 2, 3, 4" aloud over and over again, with one number per clap, speak and clap exactly with the click.

How to Clap Half Notes

1. Clap on beat 1, skip beat 2, clap on beat 3, and skip beat 4.

2. Continue clapping every other beat.

3. Count "1, 2, 3, 4" aloud as you clap.

How to Clap Whole Notes

1. Clap beat 1, then do not clap on beats 2, 3, 4.

2. You should be clapping once every 4 beats.

3. Add in the "1, 2, 3, 4" count.

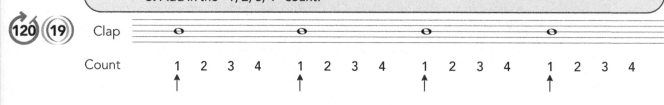

Why Clap?

We clap before we play because it is much easier than playing the piano, and that gives us more brain power to think about the rhythm. We also clap because it helps us learn the rhythm of the music before we need to think about notes, finger orders, picking, and harmony.

How to Clap Fast

To clap as fast as possible with as little tension as possible, keep your non-dominant hand flat and still as you move your dominant hand from the wrist to clap against your non-dominant hand. This technique allows for speed without unnecessary tension. If you are a rightie, your non-dominant hand is your left hand, and your dominant hand is your right hand. Lefties are the opposite.

Tempo/Time

The speed at which a piece of music is performed.

"Tempo" is an Italian word meaning "time." The word tempo is used in music to describe how slow or fast a piece of music or musical phrase should be played. It is also used when listening to a piece of music, to describe how fast it is being played.

When talking about multiple "tempos," the plural is "tempi" in formal language. More often than not, though, musicians will say "tempos."

Tempo: Listening

Tempo Examples 1

Slow	**Piano Sonata No. 14 in C-sharp minor**	Ludwig Van Beethoven
Medium	**Sweden**	C418
Fast	**Piano Man**	Billy Joel

Tempo Examples 2

Slow	**La Cathédrale Engloutie**	Claude Debussy
Medium	**Heart and Soul**	Hoagy Carmichael & Frank Loesser
Fast	**The Entertainer**	Scott Joplin

Speed Checklists

A speed checklist will help you keep track of how fast you can correctly play a song or exercise. Mark your progress with pencil in paper books and "mark up" PDF and digital copies. The numbers represent the BPM of your metronome. Not all songs and exercises will need to go to 120 BPM.

Speed checklist

50	55	60	65	70	75	75	80	85	90	95	100	105	110	115	120
○	○	○	○	○	○	○	○	○	○	○	○	○	○	○	○

Play the Notes in Time

Play the Notes in Time: Right Hand

Right Hand Finger Numbers 1 2 3 4 5

Sometimes you will find small numbers above, below, or next to some notes in the written music. These numbers tell you which finger to use to play that note. For example, when you see a "1", you play that note with you 1st finger (thumb), and when you

RH: Just in Time 1

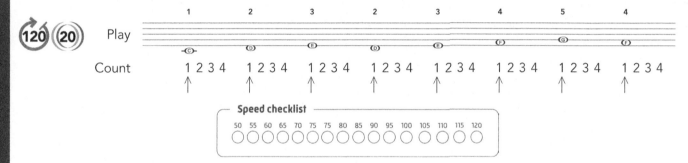

RH: Just in Time 2

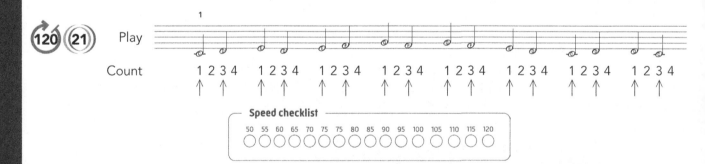

RH: Just in Time 3

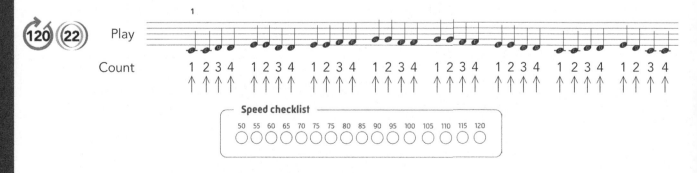

Play the Notes in Time: Left Hand

Left Hand Finger Numbers   1 2 3 4 5

Left hand finger numbers work the same way as right hand finger numbers. For example, when you see a "1", you play that note with you 1st finger (thumb), and when you see a "2", you play that note with your 2nd finger (index or pointer finger). Most of the time, left hand finger numbers are written below the staff.

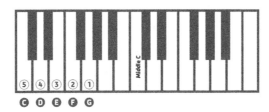

LH: Just in Time 1

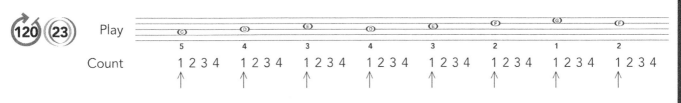

LH: Just in Time 2

LH: Just in Time 3

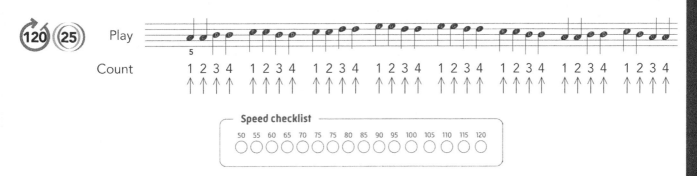

Bar Lines and Their Meanings

Bar lines divide groups of notes and chords.

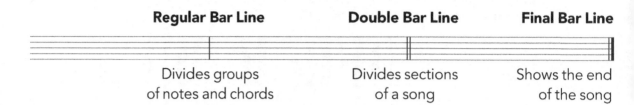

Regular Bar Line	Double Bar Line	Final Bar Line
Divides groups of notes and chords	Divides sections of a song	Shows the end of the song

Measures

Bar line   **Bar line**   **Bar line**   **Final Bar line**

A space where notes, chords and other musical notation are placed that measures time. Each measure takes place between bar lines.

- **m.** is the abbreviation of the word "measure."

The first measure has one bar line.

Measure | **Measure** | **Measure** | **Measure**

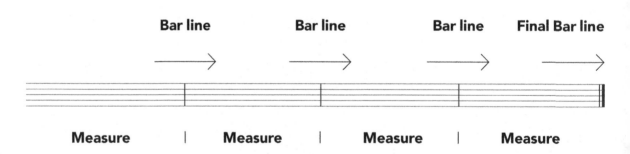

Bar line   **Bar line**   **Bar line**   **Final Bar line**

Measure | **Measure** | **Measure** | **Measure**

Bar lines always separate measures. The first measure of the song, piece of music, or exercise will not have a bar line in front of it.

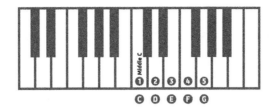

A Measured Response 1

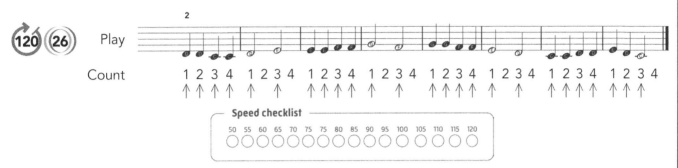

A Measured Response 2

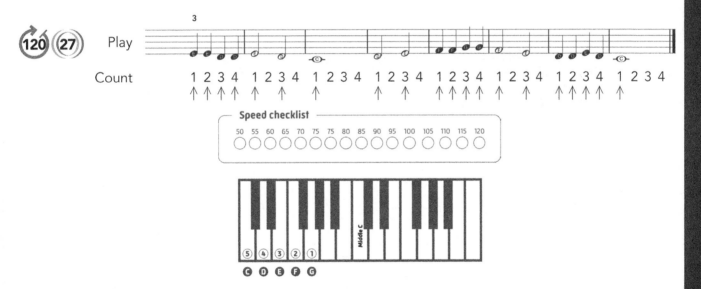

A Measured Response 3

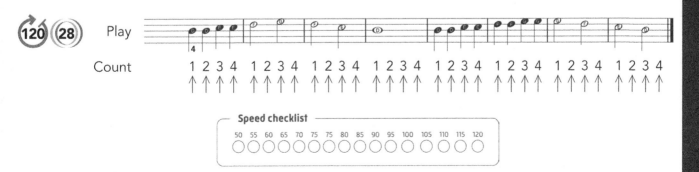

Time Signatures

$$\frac{4}{4}$$

The top number shows how many beats there are per measure. The bottom number shows the denominator of the fraction that corresponds to the name of the rhythmic value of the note.

Bottom Number	4
Bottom Number as a Fraction	¼
Name of the Fraction	Quarter
Note Value that Gets the Beat/Count	Quarter note

Top: Number of beats per measure?   Four beats per measure.

Bottom: Which type of note gets the beat? Quarter note gets the beat.

> When a note "gets the beat" it lines up with the count number and also "gets the count". Young students can focus on the top number.

Measures of 4

Measure **1st** **2nd** **3rd** **4th**

Count 1 2 3 4 1 2 3 4 1 2 3 4 1 2 3 4

Because of its popularity and common use, $\frac{4}{4}$ is sometimes written as "common time."

$$\frac{4}{4} = \mathbf{C} = \text{Common time}$$

Count 1 2 3 4 1 2 3 4 1 2 3 4 1 2 3 4

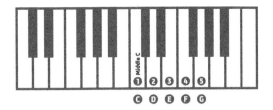

John Hancock

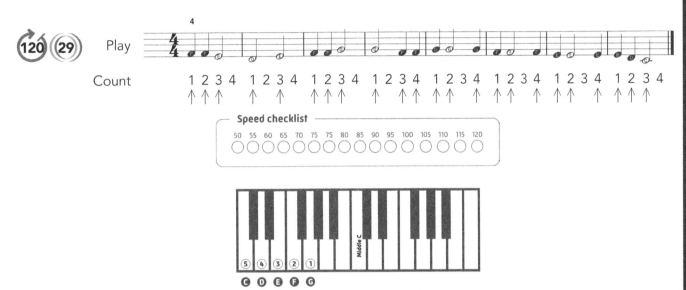

Jane Hancock

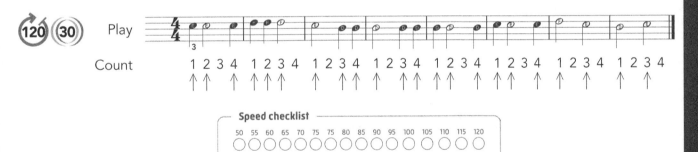

Jasara Hancock

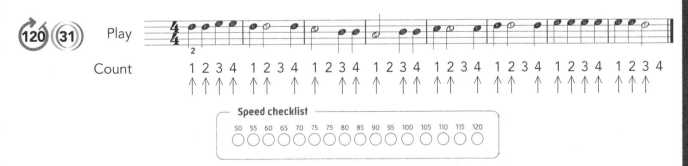

From now on quarter notes, half notes, and whole notes will not have arrows showing you where to play.

Notes on the Staff: Right Hand

- Notes are placed on the lines and spaces to indicate different pitches.

- Higher sounding pitches are towards the top of the staff (up towards the ceiling).

- Lower sounding pitches are towards the bottom of the staff (down towards the floor).

1 Line notes - lowest to highest sounding
2 Line notes - highest to lowest sounding
3 Space notes - lowest to highest sounding
4 Space notes - highest to lowest sounding

Treble Clef (G Clef): Right Hand

A symbol placed at the beginning of a staff, typically used to show notes for the right hand.

- Shows the position of the G note by curling around the G line. (that is why the treble clef is also known as the G clef).

- Shows the position of the musical alphabet on the staff based on the position of the G note.

- Resembles the letter G (it was originally a capital G).

Each line and space on the staff represents a letter of the musical alphabet. Notes marked on these lines and spaces take on the letter name that is associated with that line or space.

How to Read Notes on the Staff

Any time any note lands on a line of the staff or in the space between any two lines on the staff, it will have the same name. For example, when you see a treble clef, any note on the top line staff will always be called "F," which is why we will sometimes call the top line the "F line." Any note that is on the bottom space of the staff is always called "F," because it lands on the "F space." These are two different F notes.

All notes on this line are F
All notes on this line are D
All notes on this line are B
All notes on this line are G
All notes on this line are E

All notes in this space are E
All notes in this space are C
All notes in this space are A
All notes in this space are F

(32) How to Remember the Notes on the Staff

The note on the bottom line of the staff is E. The musical alphabet starts on E, then continues up through E again in the top space finishing on F on the top line.

High notes
Low notes

E F G A B C D E F   E G B D F   F D B G E   F A C E   E C A F

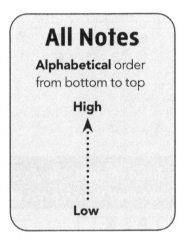
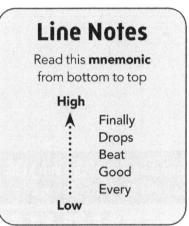
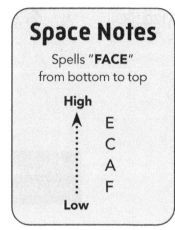

Treble Clef Ledger Lines

A short line parallel to the lines of the staff.

- Can be above or below the staff.
- Ledger lines extend the musical alphabet further from the staff, both ascending and descending.
- Used for notes that are higher or lower than the notes on the staff.
- Notice that the C and D you have been playing are both below the staff.

Ascending Ledger Lines   **Descending Ledger Lines**

(33)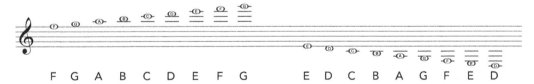

F G A B C D E F G   E D C B A G F E D

The Notes of the Treble Clef

(34)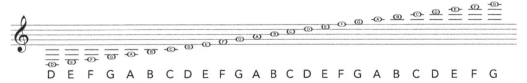

D E F G A B C D E F G A B C D E F G A B C D E F G

> From now on notes will not have their letter names written in the notehead. Memorize the notes on the staff before moving forward.

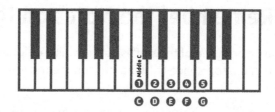

I See the Sea, C!

Best Music Coach

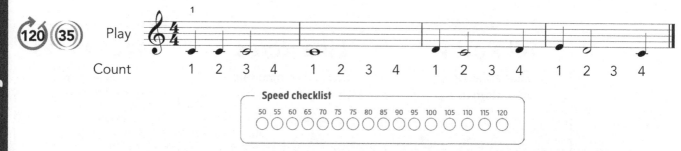

Play at a speed at which you can keep your hand relaxed. Keep your fingers just above the keys they are going to play, even when they are not playing them.

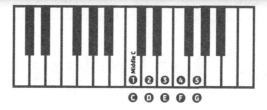

C What I Mean?

Best Music Coach

To help you keep track of the music, measure numbers are written at the beginning of each line, starting with the second line.

Keep reading and playing after the first line into the second line.

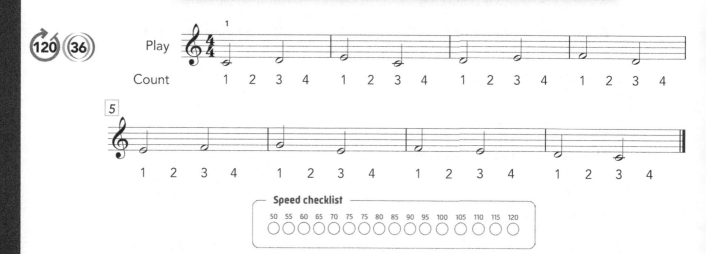

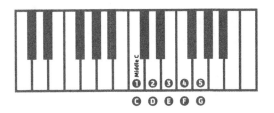

I See the Sea, C! 2

Best Music Coach

Speed checklist

50 55 60 65 70 75 75 80 85 90 95 100 105 110 115 120
○   ○   ○   ○   ○   ○   ○   ○   ○   ○   ○   ○   ○   ○   ○   ○

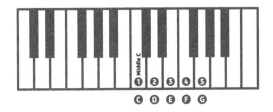

C What I Mean? 2

Best Music Coach

Speed checklist

50 55 60 65 70 75 75 80 85 90 95 100 105 110 115 120
○   ○   ○   ○   ○   ○   ○   ○   ○   ○   ○   ○   ○   ○   ○   ○

Play It and Say It!

1. Without playing, speak the names of the notes aloud through an entire song.

2. Play the song while speaking the names of the notes aloud.

Notes on the Staff: Left Hand

- Notes are placed on the lines and spaces to indicate different pitches.
- Higher sounding pitches are towards the top of the staff (up towards the ceiling).
- Lower sounding pitches are towards the bottom of the staff (down towards the floor).

1 Line notes - lowest to highest sounding
2 Line notes - highest to lowest sounding
3 Space notes - lowest to highest sounding
4 Space notes - highest to lowest sounding

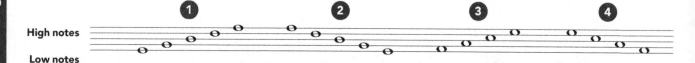

High notes

Low notes

Bass Clef (F Clef): Left Hand

A symbol placed at the beginning of a staff.
Typically shows notes for the left hand.

- Shows the position of the F note (that is why the bass clef is also known as the "F clef").
- Shows the position of the musical alphabet on the staff based on the position of the F note. The two dots of the clef show the F line.
- Resembles an old-fashioned letter F (another reason to call it the "F clef").
- Used to show lower-sounding notes than the treble staff does.
- The order of the notes on the lines and spaces of the staff is different than that on the treble clef.

F line --> 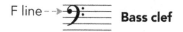 **Bass clef**

Each line and space on the staff represents a letter of the musical alphabet. Notes marked on these lines and spaces take on the letter name that is associated with that line or space.

How to Read Notes on the Staff

Any time any note lands on a line of the staff or in the space between any two lines on the staff, it will have the same name. For example, when you see a treble clef, any note on the top line staff will always be called "F," which is why we will sometimes call the top line the "F line." Any note that is on the bottom space of the staff is always called "F," because it lands on the "F space." These are two different F notes.

All notes on this line are A
All notes on this line are F
All notes on this line are D
All notes on this line are B
All notes on this line are G

All notes in this space are G
All notes in this space are E
All notes in this space are C
All notes in this space are A

(39) How to Remember the Notes on the Staff: Bass Clef

High notes

Low notes

G A B C D E F G A   G B D F A   A F D B G   A C E G   G E C A

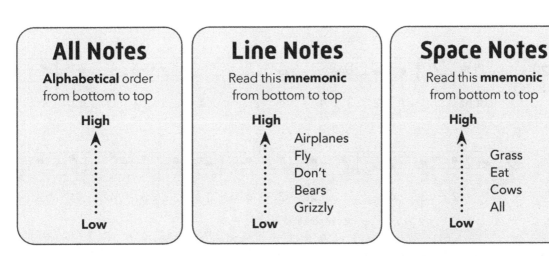

All Notes
Alphabetical order
from bottom to top

High
↑
Low

Line Notes
Read this **mnemonic**
from bottom to top

High
↑
Airplanes
Fly
Don't
Bears
Grizzly
Low

Space Notes
Read this **mnemonic**
from bottom to top

High
↑
Grass
Eat
Cows
All
Low

Tip: The left hand bass clef note mnemonics are all about animals. Remember "left hand = animals" to avoid getting confused between the right and left hands.

Bass Clef Ledger Lines

Ascending Ledger Lines   **Descending Ledger Lines**

(40)

A B C D E F G A B   G F E D C B A G F

The Notes of the Bass Clef

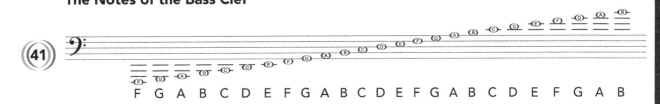

(41)

F G A B C D E F G A B C D E F G A B C D E F G A B

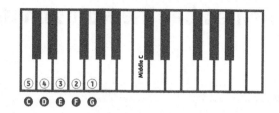

C-3PO On the Dune C

Best Music Coach

C What I Mean? 3

Best Music Coach

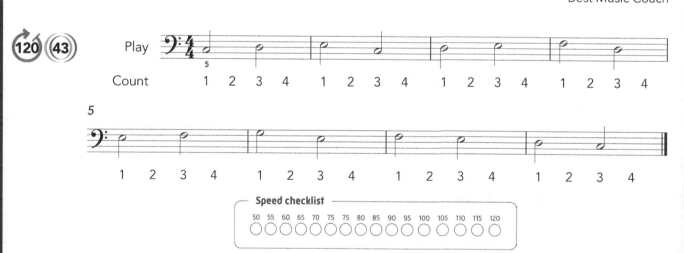

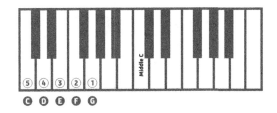

I See the Sea, C! 3

Best Music Coach

Speed checklist

50 55 60 65 70 75 75 80 85 90 95 100 105 110 115 120
○   ○   ○   ○   ○   ○   ○   ○   ○   ○   ○   ○   ○   ○   ○   ○

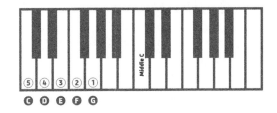

C What I Mean? 4

Best Music Coach

Speed checklist

50 55 60 65 70 75 75 80 85 90 95 100 105 110 115 120
○   ○   ○   ○   ○   ○   ○   ○   ○   ○   ○   ○   ○   ○   ○   ○

How to Practice

How you practice is just as important as what you practice. Practicing something the wrong way over and over again creates a "bad habit" that will take much more time, focus, and energy to correct.

> Practice something the right way 100 times *and* ...
> **You will play it right on the 101st time**
>
> Practice something the wrong way 100 times *and* ...
> **You will play it wrong on the 101st time**
>
> Practice something the right way 50 times and the wrong way 50 times *and* ...
> **You have a 50% chance of playing it right on the 101st time**

How to Get It Right:

- Start slow. Only play at speeds where you make no mistakes. If you start to mess up, it means you are going too fast. Slow down and try again. Gradually increase the speed over days, weeks, and months. Slow down if you start to make mistakes.

- If you make a mistake, try not to get too frustrated or angry with yourself. These emotions will probably cause you to mess up again, increasing the frustration, which will increase the amount of mistakes you make! If you start to feel frustrated, angry, impatient, or overwhelmed, put your piano down (gently) and take a break for a few minutes. Return to playing when you have had a chance to cool down your emotions.

- Stay relaxed, do not hold tension in your face, tongue, jaw, neck, shoulders, arms, wrists or hands.

- Practicing for a small amount of time every day is better than practicing for a large amount of time every other day. You will remember the songs and exercises you are learning much faster and with more accuracy with daily practice sessions. For example, 30 minutes a day is better than 1 hour every other day.

- Some students may not have the luxury of 30 minutes a day to dedicate to music. Try to carve out 5-15 minutes a day and focus on mastering one musical task before moving on to the next. Let your coach know you have time limitations and they will work with you to create a customized practice schedule that works for your schedule.

- Everyone misses a couple of days of practice here and there. Try not to feel bad about missing your practice session. Understand you may need to take a step back in your progress when you get back to practicing, but you will quickly return to where you were and continue to grow.

The Two Types of Practicing

> 1. Practicing (learning) is playing a song, or an element of music you do not know yet, or are still perfecting.
>
> 2. Practicing (playing) is reviewing a song or an element of music you know already, or making music for the fun of it.

To grow as a piano player and musician, you will use both types of practicing. It is important to remember that when you are a beginner, staying too long in the playing practice will slow your progression to becoming a better piano player and musician.

Daily Practice vs. Review Practice

As you begin practicing and playing more pieces of music, first prioritize the pieces that need active practice time, and which are "finished" and can be moved to a daily review.

Reviewing a piece you know daily for six months will greatly increase the amount of time you will remember the piece, and can even allow you to remember how to play it for the rest of your life.

How to Practice Different Pieces of Music and Exercises

Daily Practice

If what you are playing needs work, or is messy, you are unable to play at the needed speed or you are making frequent mistakes:

Dedicate daily practice time to this song or exercise.

Daily Review

If what you are playing is clean, precise, and at or above the needed speed:

Play once at the beginning or end of your practice session. If at any time you start to make mistakes while playing the review piece, song, or exercise, put it back into your daily practice until you can correct the errors in your playing. Your coach will guide you when to put songs or exercises in the Daily Review category.

Remember, if you can review a piece of music, technique, or exercise every day for six months, you may remember how to play it for the rest of your life!

Review: How to Play Your First Full Song

If any of these review points are not clear, or you can't remember what they mean, go back to the page or pages and review. Move forward in the book only when you understand and can remember all of these review points!

- Notes
  - Whole notes
  - Half notes
  - Quarter notes
- The Staff
- How to play the notes
- Key boxes
- The metronome
- Count In
- How to clap rhythms
- Tempo
- Speed checklists
- Bar lines and their meanings
- Measures
- Time signatures
- Treble clef notes
- How to read notes on the staff: treble clef
- How to remember notes on the staff
- Ledger lines
- Bass clef
- How to read notes on the staff: bass clef
- How to practice

How to Play with Both Hands

This chapter holds all the information you will need to start playing songs with both hands at the same time!

The Grand Staff

- A treble clef line of staff and bass clef line of staff joined by a brace. Find the brace.

- Music can happen on both staves at the same time.
  This means playing with both hands at the same time (more on that later).

- The grand staff is considered to be a single line of music. You will not read the treble, then bass clef lines. Rather, read them together, at the same time.

Brace

C2 D2 E2 F2 G2 A2 B2 C3 D3 E3 F3 G3 A3 B3 C4

C4 D4 E4 F4 G4 A4 B4 C5 D5 E5 F5 G5 A5 B5 C6

C Position

What is C Position?

C position is when you combine the right and left hands together to play music with the right thumb on middle C (C4) and the left pinky on C3, with all other fingers for each hand on the white keys that follow each C up to the next G.

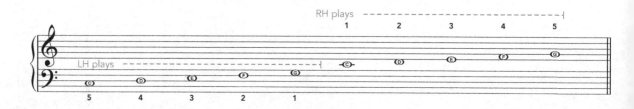

How to Play Songs with Both Hands in C Position

Look at the key box below. The right hand is playing the notes that the right hand has played so far in this book. The left hand is playing the notes that the left hand has played so far in this book. Both hands are on the piano at the same time.

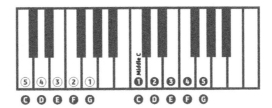

Go through this music very slowly, starting with the left hand, then playing with the right hand.

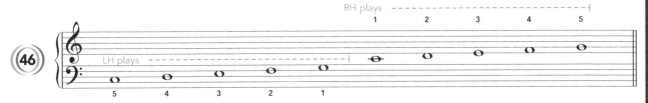

Isn't it Grand?

Best Music Coach

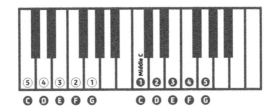

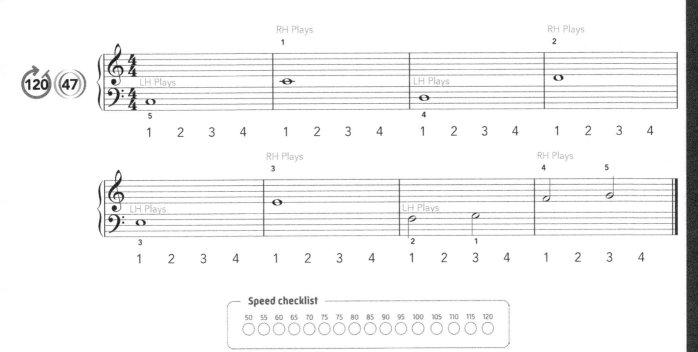

Speed checklist

50 55 60 65 70 75 75 80 85 90 95 100 105 110 115 120

Rests

A notation indicating a silence.

- Rests are silent.

- Count them, do not play them.

- When clapping, you can perform an "anti-clap" on rests. Instead of bringing your hands together, move them apart and return to a neutral position with each count of rest.

- Whole rests are equal to whole notes in duration.

- Half rests are equal to half notes in duration.

- Quarter rests are equal to quarter notes in duration.

1 Whole rest

Are "heavy" with four beats, so they "sink" below the fourth line from the bottom.

= 2 Half rests

Are "light" with two beats, so they "rise" above the third line from the bottom.

= 4 Quarter rests

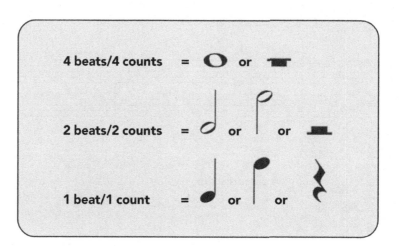

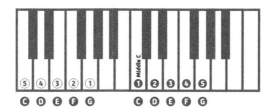

C U L8R

Best Music Coach

Speed checklist

50 55 60 65 70 75 75 80 85 90 95 100 105 110 115 120

Keep both hands curled and ready to play

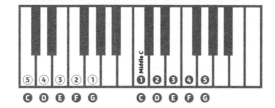

3CCC

Best Music Coach

Speed checklist

50 55 60 65 70 75 75 80 85 90 95 100 105 110 115 120

Tips for Reading Music

1. Read from left to right, top to bottom, just like a book.

2. Clap through each exercise and piece of music using a metronome before playing it on the piano.

3. Keep counting the entire time you are playing from the count in through the end of the music, either aloud or in your head.

Reading Ahead

Practice reading one note ahead of the note you are clapping or playing. Instead of looking at each note and clapping as you see it, look at the note that comes next as you clap the previous note. This allows you to "see the future" and avoid making many mistakes, because you already know what is going to happen next!

How to Read Ahead

1. Before you play or clap, look at the first note of the piece of music or exercise. Remember the note's rhythmic value and letter name.

2. Look at the second note as you play the first note. While you are playing the first note, remember the rhythmic value and letter name of the second note.

3. Look at the third note as you play the second note. While you are playing the second note, remember the rhythmic value and letter name of the third note.

Continue on in this way for the whole piece of music or exercise, keeping your eyes on the treble clef line and the bass clef line.

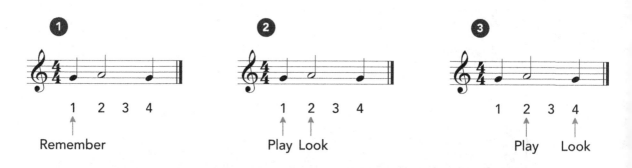

If this is difficult, try this exercise with clapping first so you only need to remember the rhythmic value and count of the notes.

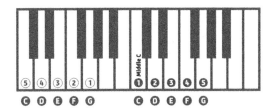

Mirror, Mirror, On the Wall

Best Music Coach

Speed checklist

50 55 60 65 70 75 75 80 85 90 95 100 105 110 115 120

You will find whole rests in two places.
1. At the beginning of measures
2. In the middle of measures
Both get four counts of silence.

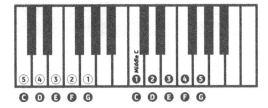

Aura Lee

George R. Poulton

This song was originally written in 1861. Almost 100 years later,
Elvis sang this melody in his song Love Me Tender.

Speed checklist

50 55 60 65 70 75 75 80 85 90 95 100 105 110 115 120

Repeat Signs

Repeat signs allow you to play the same measure, or measures, more than one time.

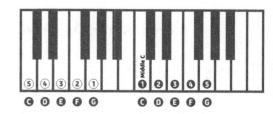

Best Music Coach

Single Repeat Sign

Déjà Vu

1. Play through the last measure.

2. Repeat back to measure 1.

3. Play through to the last measure and stop.

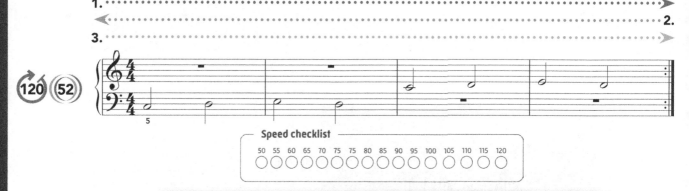

Speed checklist

50 55 60 65 70 75 75 80 85 90 95 100 105 110 115 120

> Sometimes, you will see a repeat sign at the beginning of pieces of music or songs. Repeat this once, as if it were a single repeat

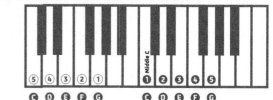

Best Music Coach

Single Repeat Sign 2

Déjà Vu 2

1. Play through the last measure.

2. Repeat back to measure 1.

3. Play through to the last measure and stop.

Speed checklist

50 55 60 65 70 75 75 80 85 90 95 100 105 110 115 120

Double Repeat Signs

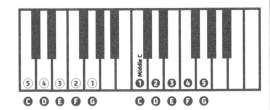

Best Music Coach

Déjà Who?

1. Play through the last measure.

2. Repeat back to the ‖: in measure 2. Do not play the first measure again.

3. Play through the last measure and stop.

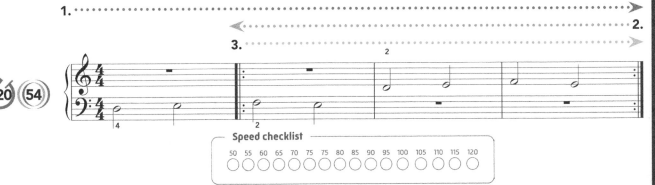

Speed checklist

50 55 60 65 70 75 75 80 85 90 95 100 105 110 115 120

Double Repeat Signs 2

Déjà You!

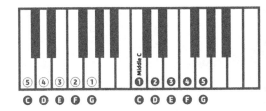

Best Music Coach

1. Play up to the :‖ in measure 7.

2. Repeat back to the ‖: in measure 2. Do not play the first measure again.

3. Play through the last measure and stop.

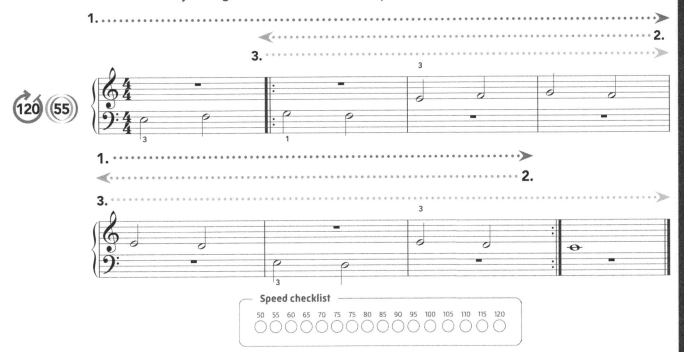

Speed checklist

50 55 60 65 70 75 75 80 85 90 95 100 105 110 115 120

How to Play with Both Hands at the Same Time

Playing with both hands at the same time accurately and with good technique can be tricky to do. Go slowly and carefully through this exercise, watching your technique – that is, keeping your fingers gently curled. When you play two notes together at the same time it is a dyad, also called an "interval."

The goal is for the notes that you play together with both hands to sound at exactly the same time. One should not sound before the other. Time your fingers and how you press down the keys to get a clean sound.

Together, Forever, Until the End of Time

Best Music Coach

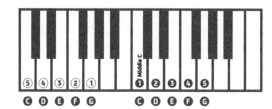

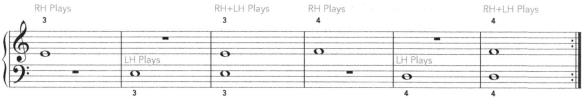

(57) Hear the Difference: Left Hand Rush, Right Hand Rush, Together

When you play a note too early, or a song, or exercise too fast, we can call this "rushing," Listen to the examples and see if you can hear the difference between the notes that are together, and the notes where one hand is rushing ahead of the other.

In "Together, Forever, Until the End of Time 2" you will see the left and right hands sharing measures for the first time! This is the longest song you have played so far!

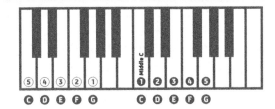

Together, Forever, Until the End of Time 2

Best Music Coach

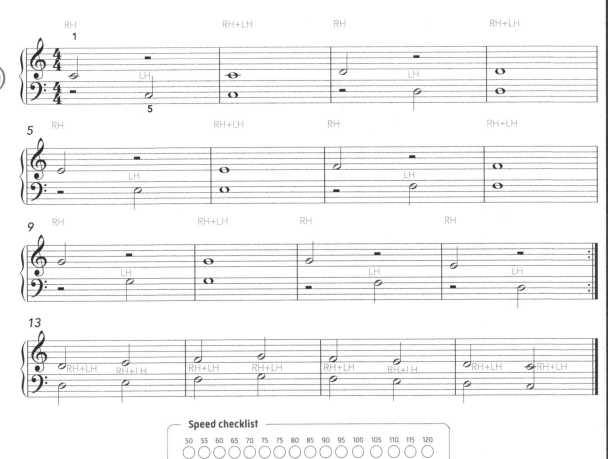

We want to hear from you and empower you to become a great piano player! Upload videos of yourself playing exercises and songs from this book to any social media platform + tag @bestmusiccoach for reshares/retweets, free tips, free feedback, and shoutouts!

How to Practice Songs that use Two Hands

Here are some tips for getting started playing songs and exercises with both hands.

> **1.** Learn just the right-h and part by itself.
>
> **2.** Learn just the left-hand part by itself.
>
> **3.** Play both hands together slowly.
>
> **4.** Keep playing slowly until you can play through the piece with correct technique.

Together, Forever, Until the End of Time 3

Best Music Coach

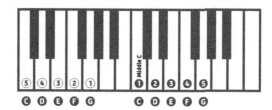

Speed checklist

50 55 60 65 70 75 75 80 85 90 95 100 105 110 115 120
◯ ◯ ◯ ◯ ◯ ◯ ◯ ◯ ◯ ◯ ◯ ◯ ◯ ◯ ◯ ◯

From now on you will not see finger number reminders for C position, until you learn to switch positions!

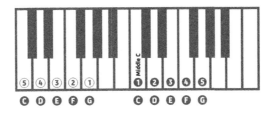

How to Make Friends

Best Music Coach

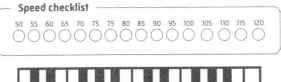

C Spot Run

Best Music Coach

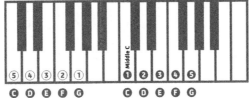

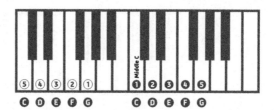

C Horses

Best Music Coach

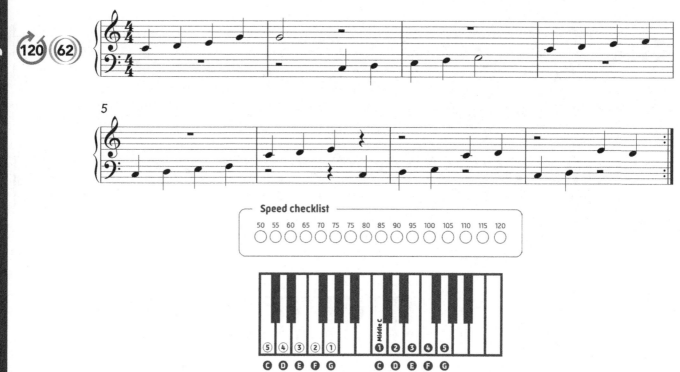

Speed checklist

50 55 60 65 70 75 75 80 85 90 95 100 105 110 115 120

Two-hand Étude

Best Music Coach

An étude (ay-tood) is a study of some part of music. Étude is a French word that means "study".

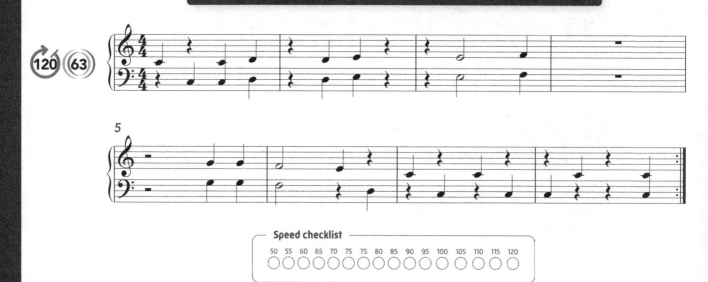

Speed checklist

50 55 60 65 70 75 75 80 85 90 95 100 105 110 115 120

A New Time Signature: $\frac{3}{4}$

In "three, four" time, there are three quarter notes in each measure. The quarter note still gets the "beat," meaning that you will count the quarter notes as "one, two, three."

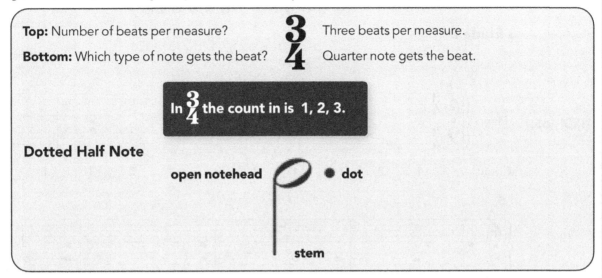

Top: Number of beats per measure? **$\frac{3}{4}$** Three beats per measure.

Bottom: Which type of note gets the beat? Quarter note gets the beat.

In $\frac{3}{4}$ the count in is 1, 2, 3.

Dotted Half Note

open notehead • dot

stem

Dotted Notes

Dotted notes are worth 1 $\frac{1}{2}$ times the written note's rhythmic value.
The written note value + $\frac{1}{2}$ of the written note value = dotted note value

To perform a dotted half note, attack the string on beat/count 1, skip down on beats 2 and 3.

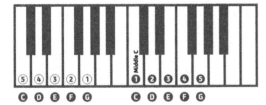

In $\frac{3}{4}$ whole rests get 3 counts of silence.

3 Étude

Best Music Coach

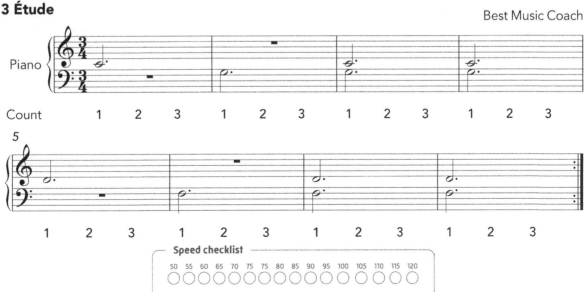

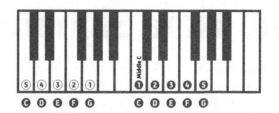

3 Étude 2

Best Music Coach

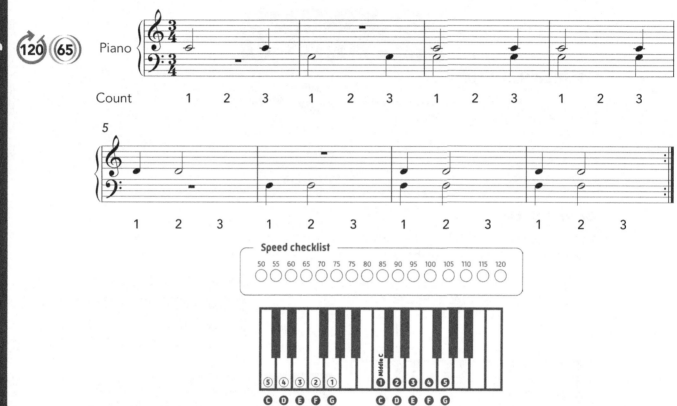

120 65

Piano

Count 1 2 3 1 2 3 1 2 3 1 2 3

5

1 2 3 1 2 3 1 2 3 1 2 3

Speed checklist
50 55 60 65 70 75 75 80 85 90 95 100 105 110 115 120

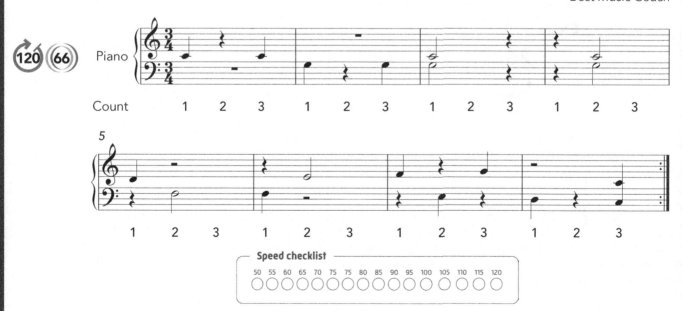

3 Étude 3

Best Music Coach

120 66

Piano

Count 1 2 3 1 2 3 1 2 3 1 2 3

5

1 2 3 1 2 3 1 2 3 1 2 3

Speed checklist
50 55 60 65 70 75 75 80 85 90 95 100 105 110 115 120

**This is the first time you will play different rhythms in each hand.
Remember to hold each note down for all the counts that it gets!**

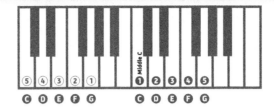

3 Étude 4

Best Music Coach

Piano

Count   1   2   3   1   2   3   1   2   3   1   2   3

1   2   3   1   2   3   1   2   3   1   2   3

Speed checklist
50 55 60 65 70 75 75 80 85 90 95 100 105 110 115 120
○   ○   ○   ○   ○   ○   ○   ○   ○   ○   ○   ○   ○   ○   ○   ○

3 Étude 5

Best Music Coach

Piano

Count   1   2   3   1   2   3   1   2   3   1   2   3

1   2   3   1   2   3   1   2   3   1   2   3

Speed checklist
50 55 60 65 70 75 75 80 85 90 95 100 105 110 115 120
○   ○   ○   ○   ○   ○   ○   ○   ○   ○   ○   ○   ○   ○   ○   ○

Review: How to Play with Both Hands

If any of these review points are not clear, or you can't remember what they mean, go back to the page or pages and review. Move forward in the book only when you understand and can remember all of these review points!

- The grand staff
- C position
- Rests
    - Whole rests
    - Half rests
    - Quarter rests
- Tips for reading music
- Repeat signs
    - Single repeat signs
    - Double repeat signs
- How to play with both hands at the same time
- Hear the difference between together and rushing
- How to practice songs that use two hands
- A new time signature:

If you feel like you have learned anything helpful from this book, please leave a 5-star review to help other people just like you find this book and experience the joy of making music!

Please leave a review

Middle C Position

This chapter holds all the information you will need to start playing songs with both hands in middle C position!

Middle C Position

What is Middle C Position?

Middle C position is when you combine the right and left hands together to play music with the right thumb on middle C (C4) and the left hand thumb also on middle C (C4).

How to Play Songs with Both Hands in Middle C Position

Look at the key box below. The right hand is playing the notes that the right hand has played so far in this book. The left hand is playing F, G, A, B and C. Look at the new notes below. Memorize the names and placements of the new notes before moving forward.

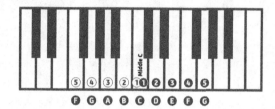

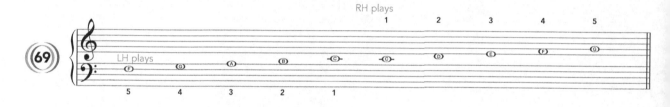

Learn the Left Hand

Best Music Coach

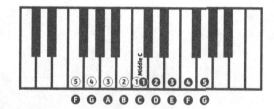

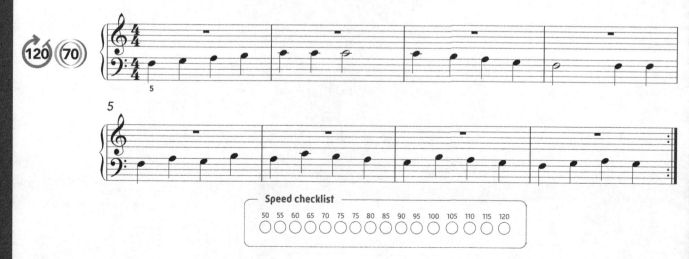

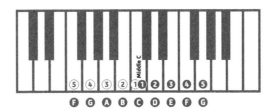

Middle C Étude 1

Best Music Coach

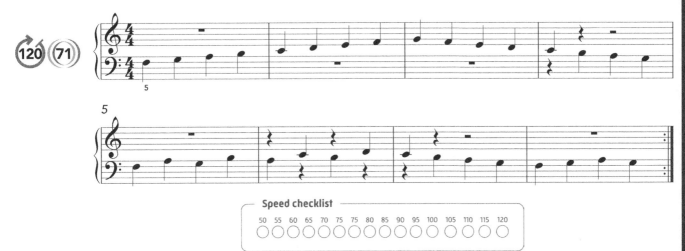

Middle C Étude 2

Best Music Coach

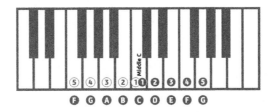

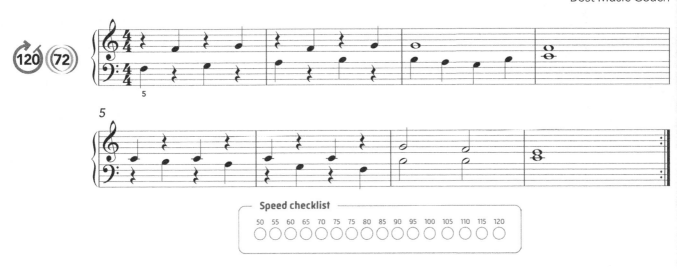

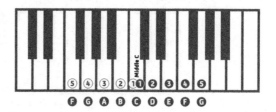

Mais, Oui! Ceci c'est C!

Best Music Coach

Speed checklist

50 55 60 65 70 75 75 80 85 90 95 100 105 110 115 120
◯ ◯ ◯ ◯ ◯ ◯ ◯ ◯ ◯ ◯ ◯ ◯ ◯ ◯ ◯ ◯

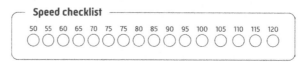

¡Si, Esta es una Siesta C!

Best Music Coach

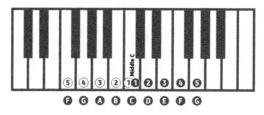

Speed checklist

50 55 60 65 70 75 75 80 85 90 95 100 105 110 115 120
◯ ◯ ◯ ◯ ◯ ◯ ◯ ◯ ◯ ◯ ◯ ◯ ◯ ◯ ◯ ◯

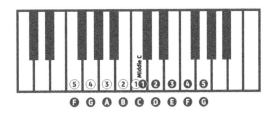

Resting

Best Music Coach

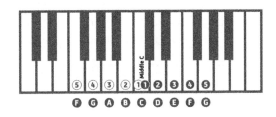

Symmetry

Best Music Coach

C My Tree?

Speed checklist

50 55 60 65 70 75 75 80 85 90 95 100 105 110 115 120
○   ○   ○   ○   ○   ○   ○   ○   ○   ○   ○   ○   ○   ○   ○   ○

Review: Middle C Position

If any of these review points are not clear, or you can't remember what they mean, go back to the page or pages and review. Move forward in the book only when you understand and can remember all of these review points!

- Middle C position
- What is Middle C Position?
- How to Play Songs with Both Hands in Middle C Position

How to Switch Positions

Learn to switch between C position and Middle C position! This chapter is to prepare you to start playing Level 1: Notation songs in C!

How to Change Positions During a Song

Many songs will require your hands to be in more than one position during the song.

> **Tips for position changing:**
>
> 1. Practice moving your hand back and forth between the two positions without playing any notes. Get a feel for the distance and how the piano keys feel under your fingers.
>
> 2. Try to memorize the feeling of the hand movement from one position to the next.
>
> 3. At first, look where you are going. Visualize what your hand will look like in the new position before moving it, then move!

What is C Position + Middle C Position?

Middle C position is when you combine the right and left hands together to play music with the right thumb on middle C (C4) and the left hand moves between C Position and Middle C Position.

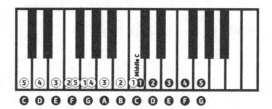

How to Cross Fingers

Why Cross Fingers?

Crossing fingers is a great way to move between keys and allows your hand to move freely around the piano playing any key, instead of being stuck in one position. Sometimes you will cross fingers, sometimes you will just pick your hand up and move it.

> **How to Cross Fingers**
>
> 1. Keep your wrist flat, do not turn or torque your wrist.
>
> 2. Cross over or under the correct fingers without introducing tension into your hand, wrist or arm.
>
> 3. Use the smallest movement possible to execute the technique.
>
> 4. From low-note keys to high-note keys, LH crosses over with 3rd or 4th fingers.
>
> 5. From high-note keys to low-note keys, LH crosses under with 1st finger.

LH Cross Over (Low to High)

1 LH 1st finger plays a key.

2 LH 1st finger stays on the key. LH 3rd finger crosses over to reach the next key to the right.

3 Move LH 1st finger out from beneath the hand

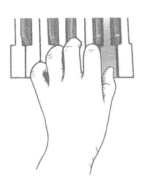
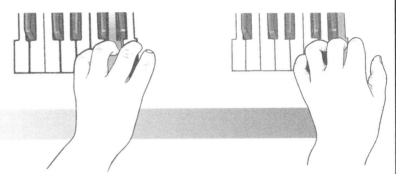

LH Cross Under (High to Low)

3 Move LH 3rd finger across and over the 1st finger.

2 LH 3rd finger stays on the key. LH 1st finger crosses under the hand to reach the next key to the left

1 LH 3rd finger plays plays a key.

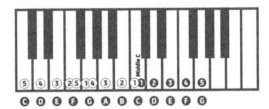

From C to Shining C

Best Music Coach

C Position   Middle C Position

C Position   Middle C Position

Speed checklist
50 55 60 65 70 75 75 80 85 90 95 100 105 110 115 120

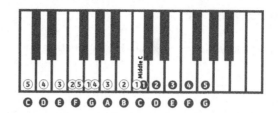

I CAN C IT!

Best Music Coach

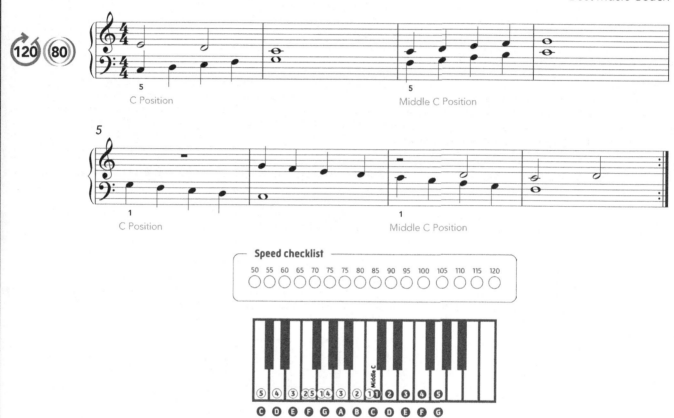

Speed checklist

50 55 60 65 70 75 75 80 85 90 95 100 105 110 115 120
◯ ◯ ◯ ◯ ◯ ◯ ◯ ◯ ◯ ◯ ◯ ◯ ◯ ◯ ◯ ◯

C Thru

Best Music Coach

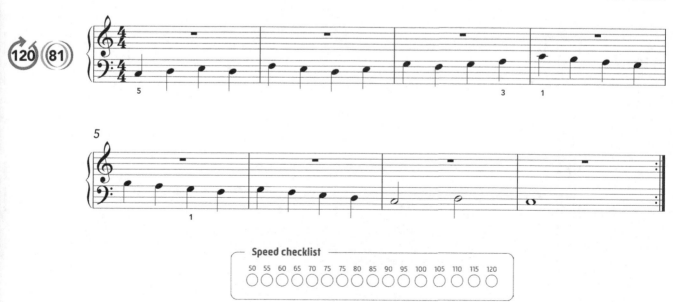

Speed checklist

50 55 60 65 70 75 75 80 85 90 95 100 105 110 115 120
◯ ◯ ◯ ◯ ◯ ◯ ◯ ◯ ◯ ◯ ◯ ◯ ◯ ◯ ◯ ◯

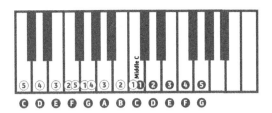

C What I Mean? 5

Best Music Coach

Speed checklist

50 55 60 65 70 75 75 80 85 90 95 100 105 110 115 120

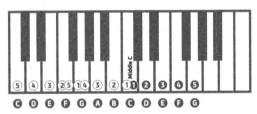

C is for CrissCross

Best Music Coach

Speed checklist

50 55 60 65 70 75 75 80 85 90 95 100 105 110 115 120

Tied Notes

Tied notes are worth the value of both the notes connected by the tie. Ties can connect notes in a measure, from one measure to the next, and from one line (staff) to the next. To make room for ties and other music symbols, the treble clef staff and bass clef staff will be further apart from each other from now on. All positions, notes, and finger numbers remain the same.

Tie

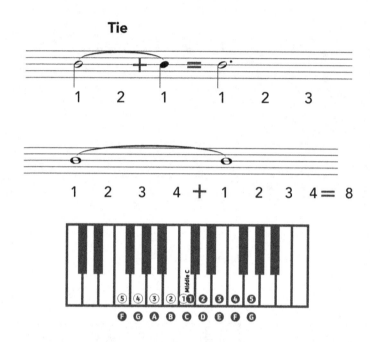

Tie, Tie Étude

> In Tie, Tie Étude the count is in black and the total counts for each pair of tied notes is in gray.

Best Music Coach

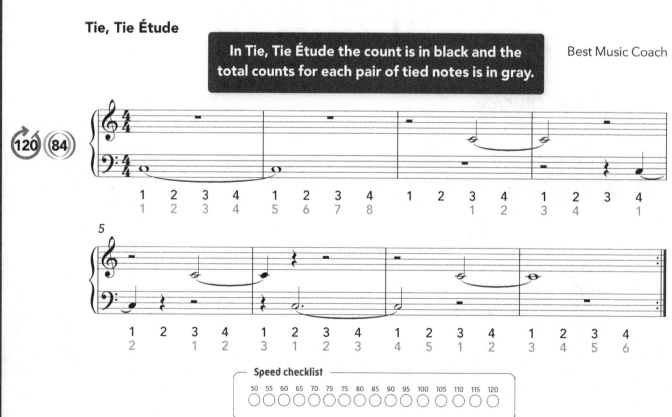

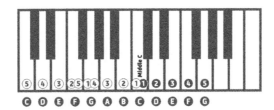

Building Bridges

Best Music Coach

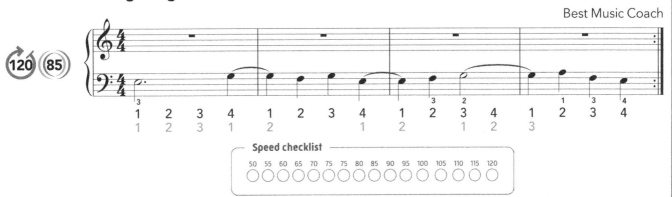

In Off-Balance, try to keep the melody smooth as it moves between the right and left hand. It should sound like one hand is playing.

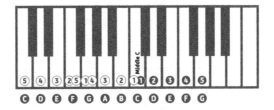

Off-Balance

Best Music Coach

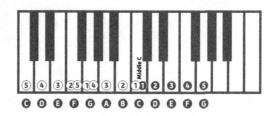

Firelight

Best Music Coach

Speed checklist

50 55 60 65 70 75 75 80 85 90 95 100 105 110 115 120

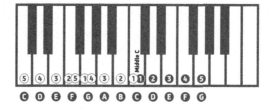

The Story So Far

Best Music Coach

Speed checklist

50 55 60 65 70 75 75 80 85 90 95 100 105 110 115 120

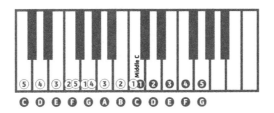

And Then...

Best Music Coach

Speed checklist

50	55	60	65	70	75	75	80	85	90	95	100	105	110	115	120
○	○	○	○	○	○	○	○	○	○	○	○	○	○	○	○

But Wait...

Best Music Coach

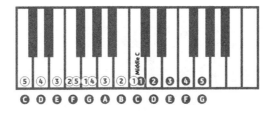

Speed checklist

50	55	60	65	70	75	75	80	85	90	95	100	105	110	115	120
○	○	○	○	○	○	○	○	○	○	○	○	○	○	○	○

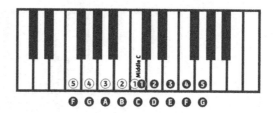

Rest a While

Best Music Coach

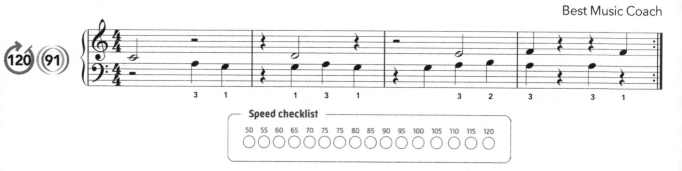

Speed checklist

50 55 60 65 70 75 75 80 85 90 95 100 105 110 115 120
◯ ◯ ◯ ◯ ◯ ◯ ◯ ◯ ◯ ◯ ◯ ◯ ◯ ◯ ◯ ◯

Review: How to Switch Positions

If any of these review points are not clear, or you can't remember what they mean, go back to the page or pages and review. Move forward in the book only when you understand and can remember all of these review points!

- How to change positions during a song
- C position + middle C position
- Left hand crossover
    3rd finger over
    1st finger under
- Tied notes

Chords

Chords (harmony) are the combination of at least two different notes sounding together at the same time. When you play two or more notes at the same time (harmony) on the piano, it is called a chord.

Two-Note Chords (Dyads)

When there are two notes in a chord, it is called a dyad, or an interval depending on who you ask (it is a long story). For now, we will call them dyads. You have already played dyads in previous chapters with one note in each hand. Sometimes when notes are close together, the noteheads will face different directions.

What is an "Attack" in Music?

Whenever you start to play a note or chord it is called an "attack". This word may seem aggressive, but is actually correct for playing music, and can be found in the dictionary!
When the notes of a chord are attacked at slightly different times, the chord no longer sounds like a single piece of sound. When you play chords you should never hear two separate attacks. You should hear with your ears and feel with your fingers that all notes of the chord are attacked at the same exact moment.

Hear the Difference: Together, Early/Late

 Hear the difference between when the notes of a chord are attacked together, and when the attack is one note is early or late.

1. All notes together

2. One note early

3. All notes together

4. One note late

5. All notes together

How to Play Chords

1. Prepare your fingers above the keys you need to play to perform the chord.

2. Allow your arm weight to drop down as you play the chord. Keep your fingers and hand shape gently locked in place, so that all notes sound together at the same time.

3. Let the weight of your arms be absorbed in your wrists.

4. Keep the keys of the chord notes held down.

5. Let your wrist float up and release the notes.

All keys of the chord must be played at exactly the same time. No notes should stand out or happen before or after the other notes of the chord.

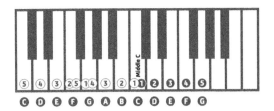

Chords 1

Best Music Coach

Speed checklist

50 55 60 65 70 75 75 80 85 90 95 100 105 110 115 120
○ ○ ○ ○ ○ ○ ○ ○ ○ ○ ○ ○ ○ ○ ○ ○

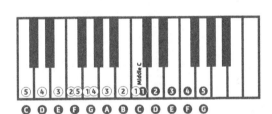

Chords 2

Best Music Coach

Speed checklist

50 55 60 65 70 75 75 80 85 90 95 100 105 110 115 120
○ ○ ○ ○ ○ ○ ○ ○ ○ ○ ○ ○ ○ ○ ○ ○

Go back and Listen to "Hear the Difference: Together, Early/Late" as many times as you need to until you can clearly hear in your own playing when your attacks are together or early/late.

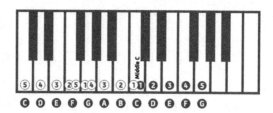

Chords and Notes 1

Best Music Coach

Speed checklist

50 55 60 65 70 75 80 85 90 95 100 105 110 115 120

Chords and Notes 2

Best Music Coach

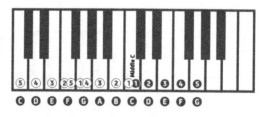

Speed checklist

50 55 60 65 70 75 80 85 90 95 100 105 110 115 120

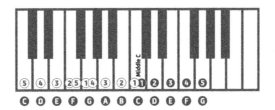

Poché Burl's Camera

Best Music Coach

Speed checklist

50 55 60 65 70 75 75 80 85 90 95 100 105 110 115 120

Three-Note Chords (Triads)

When there are three particular notes in a chord, it is called a triad. Not all three note chords are triads, but for now, all the three note chords that you see will be triads.

New Notes for the Left Hand

These new notes are an extension of C position. To play the A note one above G, extend the 1st finger (of your left hand) one white key to the right. To play the B note one below C, extend your 5th finger one white key to the left. Memorize the names and placements of the new notes before moving forward.

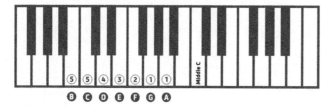

New Chords for the Left Hand

All triads have names. To learn more about why the triads are named the way they are, please see *The Best Music Theory Book for Beginners 1*.

C Major LH

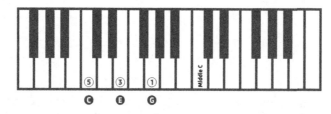
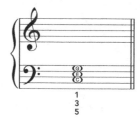

F Major LH

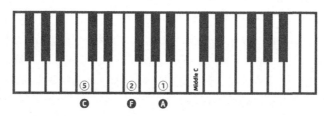
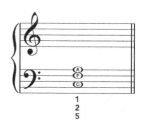

(101) G Major LH

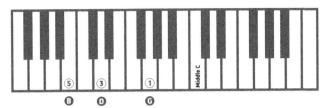
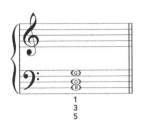

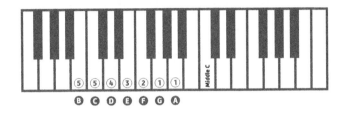

Where's Dinner?

Best Music Coach

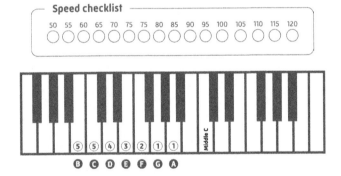

What's for Dinner?

Best Music Coach

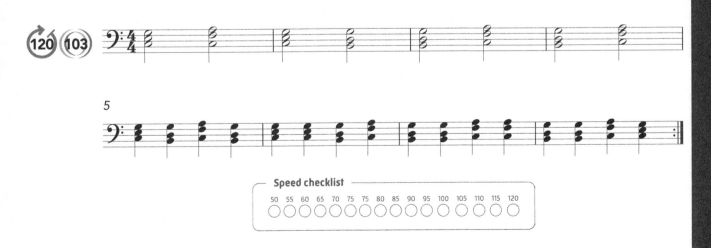

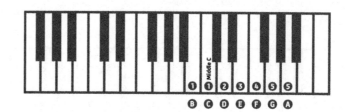

New Notes for the Right Hand

These new notes are an extension of C position. To play the B note below middle C, extend the 1st finger (of your right hand) one white key to the left. To play the A note above G, extend your 5th finger one white key to the right. Memorize the names and placements of the new notes before moving forward.

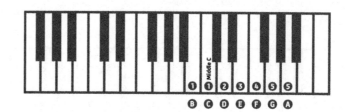

RH plays

(104)

New Chords for the Right Hand

(105) C Major RH

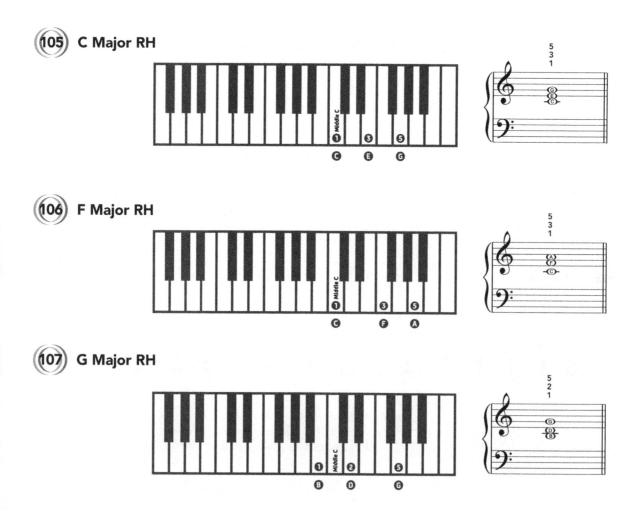

(106) F Major RH

(107) G Major RH

Reminder: All keys of the chord must be played at exactly the same time. No notes should stand out or happen before or after the other notes of the chord.

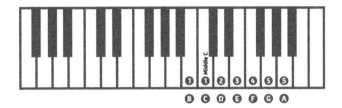

Who's for Dinner?

Best Music Coach

Speed checklist

50 55 60 65 70 75 75 80 85 90 95 100 105 110 115 120

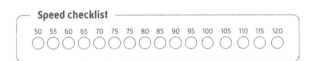

OM NOM NOM

Best Music Coach

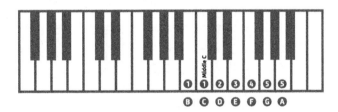

Speed checklist

50 55 60 65 70 75 75 80 85 90 95 100 105 110 115 120

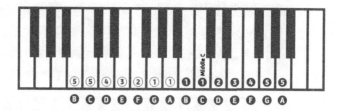

Try Two Triads

Best Music Coach

Speed checklist

50 55 60 65 70 75 75 80 85 90 95 100 105 110 115 120

Touting Triads Took Tries to Take Two Towers!

Best Music Coach

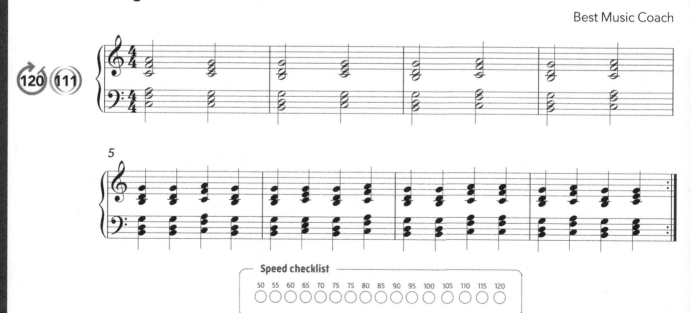

Speed checklist

50 55 60 65 70 75 75 80 85 90 95 100 105 110 115 120

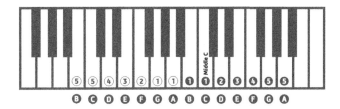

Notes and Chords and

Speed checklist
50 55 60 65 70 75 75 80 85 90 95 100 105 110 115 120
○ ○ ○ ○ ○ ○ ○ ○ ○ ○ ○ ○ ○ ○ ○ ○

Chords and Notes and

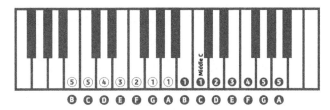

Speed checklist
50 55 60 65 70 75 75 80 85 90 95 100 105 110 115 120
○ ○ ○ ○ ○ ○ ○ ○ ○ ○ ○ ○ ○ ○ ○ ○

Chords

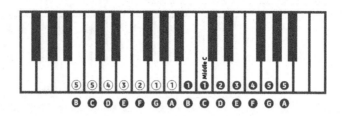

Switcheroonies

Best Music Coach

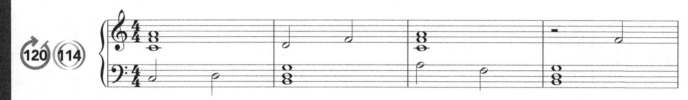

Speed checklist

50 55 60 65 70 75 75 80 85 90 95 100 105 110 115 120
○ ○ ○ ○ ○ ○ ○ ○ ○ ○ ○ ○ ○ ○ ○ ○

Switcheroonies 2

Best Music Coach

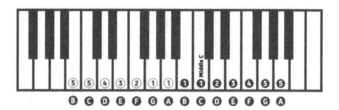

Speed checklist

50 55 60 65 70 75 75 80 85 90 95 100 105 110 115 120
○ ○ ○ ○ ○ ○ ○ ○ ○ ○ ○ ○ ○ ○ ○ ○

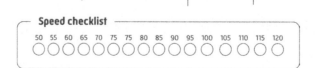

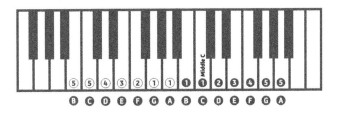

Switcheroonies 3

Best Music Coach

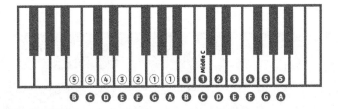

Switcheroonies 4

Best Music Coach

Chord Review

If any of these review points are not clear, or you can't remember what they mean, go back to the page or pages and review. Move forward in the book only when you understand and can remember all of these review points!

- Two-note chords (dyads)
- Attack
- Hear the difference: together, early/late
- How to play chords
- Three-note chords (triads)
    - C major
    - F major
    - G major
- New notes: B, A

Now you can play all the Level 1: Notation songs in C Major! Pick any song that has the C Major and piano tag! www.bestsheetmusic.com

G Position

To play in G position you will be moving your hands to a different place on the keyboard. After the next chapter you will have the tools to play all Level 1: Notation songs!.

G Position

G position is when your right hand 1st finger plays the G above middle C and the left hand can be in one of two places:

1. The G below middle C

2. 2 Gs below middle C

All the Notes in G Position

Memorize the names and placements of the new notes before moving forward.

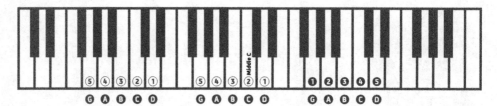

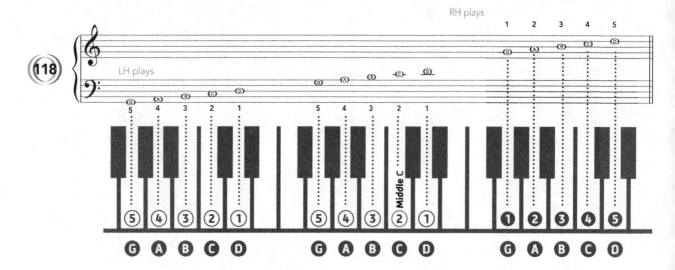

Learn the Hands

Best Music Coach

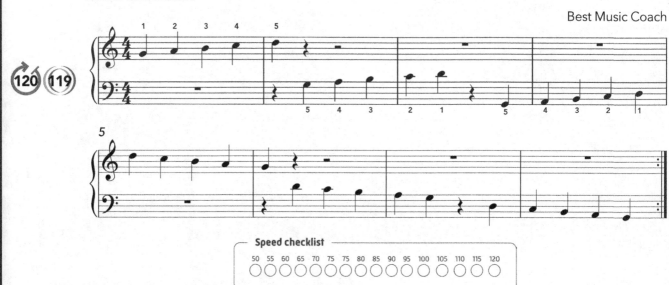

Speed checklist

50 55 60 65 70 75 75 80 85 90 95 100 105 110 115 120

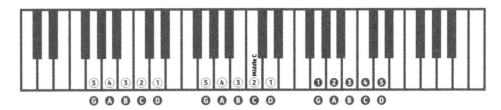

Go Get Going!

Best Music Coach

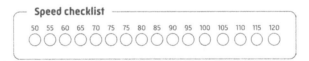

Speed checklist

50 55 60 65 70 75 75 80 85 90 95 100 105 110 115 120

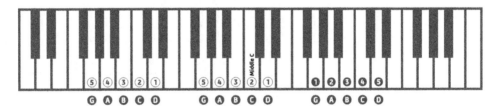

Great Gargantuan Goldfish

Best Music Coach

Speed checklist

50 55 60 65 70 75 75 80 85 90 95 100 105 110 115 120

Glenda Greets Garry

Best Music Coach

Speed checklist

50 55 60 65 70 75 75 80 85 90 95 100 105 110 115 120

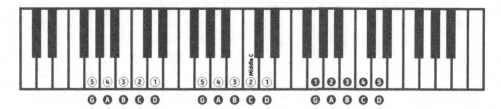

Gary Goes Golfing

Best Music Coach

Speed checklist

50 55 60 65 70 75 75 80 85 90 95 100 105 110 115 120

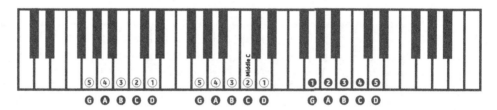

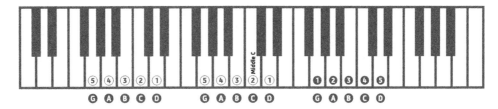

Glenda Gets Gyrostabilizers

Best Music Coach

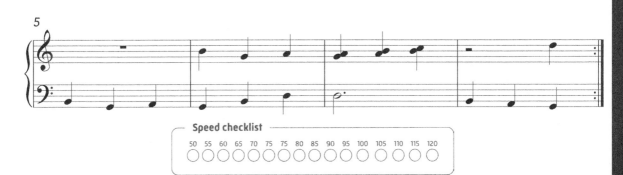

Speed checklist

50 55 60 65 70 75 75 80 85 90 95 100 105 110 115 120

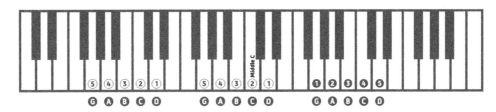

Good Grief Grant!

Best Music Coach

Speed checklist

50 55 60 65 70 75 75 80 85 90 95 100 105 110 115 120

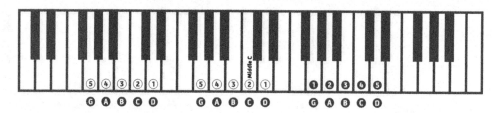

Gary, Glenda, Grant go for Gold!

Best Music Coach

Speed checklist

50 55 60 65 70 75 75 80 85 90 95 100 105 110 115 120
○   ○   ○   ○   ○   ○   ○   ○   ○   ○   ○   ○   ○   ○   ○   ○

Review: G Position

If any of these review points are not clear, or you can't remember what they mean, go back to the page or pages and review. Move forward in the book only when you understand and can remember all of these review points!

- What is G position?
- All the notes in G position

Music Theory & Chords

In this chapter you will learn a little bit about music theory and how you can use it to play the piano. After completing this chapter you will have the tools you need to play all Level 1: Notation songs!

Accidentals

A musical symbol that raises or lowers a note or returns the raised or lowered note to its natural state.

- The note that is raised, lowered, or returned to its natural state can also be called an accidental.

- You will see accidentals in several forms in this and other Best Music Coach books. This is to prepare you for encountering accidentals in different fonts and handwritings in the real world!

♮ Natural

Returns a flat (lowered) or sharp (raised) note to its original state.

"Natural" is added to the note name.

Say: "A natural."

Sharp

Makes the note sound at a higher pitch.

"Sharp" is added to the note name.

Say: "A sharp."

F   F#   F♮

Any accidental effects all instances of the same note on the same line until the end of the measure, or until a "natural" sign cancels the accidental. A note with an accidental can tie into the following measure and remains changed by the accidental. The accidental does NOT change notes in both hands, only the line of staff it is written on.

How to Play Sharp Notes

1. Play a F note with RH 4th finger and LH 2nd finger. These are F (F natural) notes.

2. Play the black key to the right of the F key. This is a F# note. Play it with RH 4th finger and LH 2nd finger. These are both F# ("F sharp") notes.

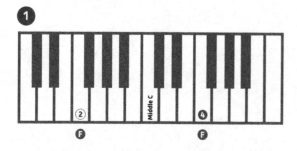

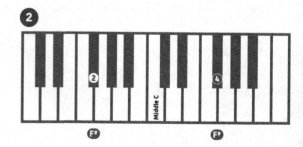

F♯

Pitch Class

All the notes that share the same name are called a "pitch class." A pitch class means the letter name of all the notes that share the same name, both high and low. All the F♯'s are a pitch class. All B's, C's, D's, G's, and so on are each a pitch class.

The accidental only changes the note for the measure it is in. Following measures may have a reminder natural sign or "courtesy accidental" to remind you how to play the note.

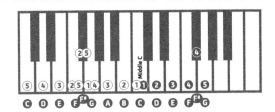

Fielding Fs

Best Music Coach

courtesy accidental

courtesy accidental

courtesy accidental

Speed checklist

50 55 60 65 70 75 75 80 85 90 95 100 105 110 115 120

Fielding Fs 2

Best Music Coach

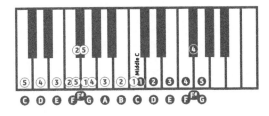

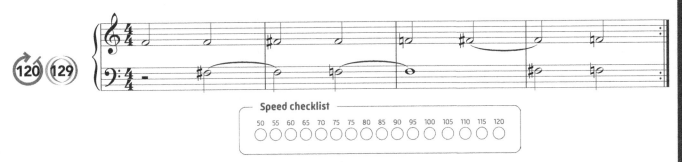

Speed checklist

50 55 60 65 70 75 75 80 85 90 95 100 105 110 115 120

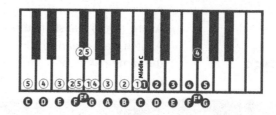

Okay, Now I'm Confused

Best Music Coach

Speed checklist
50 55 60 65 70 75 75 80 85 90 95 100 105 110 115 120

Key Signatures

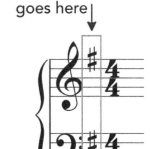

key signature goes here ↓

- Placed between the clef and the time signature.

- Use sharps, flats, and the absence of sharps and flats to indicate the key of a piece of music.

- When an accidental is on a line or space, it changes all notes that share the name of that line or space. For example: F♯ in the key signature means all Fs are to be played and read as F♯s. B♭ in the key signature means all Bs are to be played and read as B♭.

Incorrect
No accidentals needed for any F♯, because there is an F♯ in the key signature.

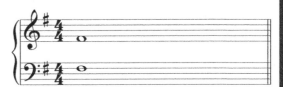

Correct
Because there is an F♯ in the key signature, all F notes on every line and space are sharp. All F notes are now played and read as F♯ unless changed by an accidental.

How to Read Music with a Key Signature

1. Remember to look for a key signature **before** you start playing!

2. Remember that all notes that share the same letter name (the pitch class) will be changed by the key signature.

3. The key signature does not show an accidental on every line or space where the pitch class can go.

4. Courtesy accidentals can remind you of the accidentals in the key signature.

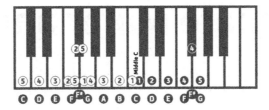

The Key

Best Music Coach

Music Theory & Chords

D Major Chord Both Hands

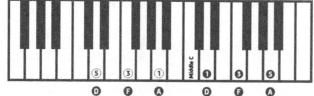

D Minor Chord Both Hands

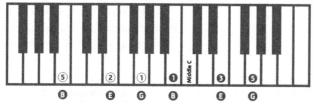

E Minor Chord Both Hands

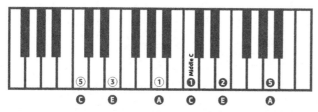
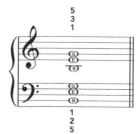

A Minor Chord Both Hands

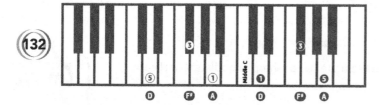
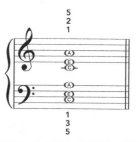

In real-life situations and songs, you will come across many chords that are two or three-note combinations and variations taken from chords you already know.

Compare Major and Minor

Major chords have a happy, easy sound. Minor chords have a sad, thoughtful sound. Compare the sounds of your D major and D minor chords. Can you hear that the D major chord sounds happy? Can you hear that the D minor chord sounds sad?

Major

Emotion?
Happy

Minor

Emotion?
Sad

Backing Tracks

The video example for "Graduation Song" is a play-along track called a "backing track". Listen to the four, count in clicks in the example, and then play along with the track! You may need to practice this song with a metronome at first to get it up to 120 BPM. You will see the backing track icon from now on when an example uses a backing track. Look out for those back-to-back repeat signs. Play measures 1-4 two times. Then play measures 5-8 two times before playing measure 9.

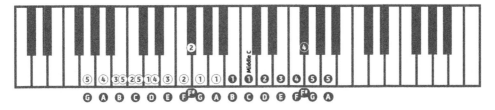

Graduation Song!

Best Music Coach

Review: Music Theory & Chords

If any of these review points are not clear, or you can't remember what they mean, go back to the page or pages and review. Move forward in the book only when you understand and can remember all of these review points!

- Accidentals
    Natural
    Sharp

- How to play sharp notes

- F#

- Pitch class

- Key signatures

- How to read music with a key signature

- Chords
    D major
    D minor
    E minor
    A minor

- Compare major and minor

- Backing tracks

Now you can play all the Level 1: Notation songs! www.bestsheetmusic.com

How to Play Your Favorie Songs

How to Read Leadsheets

Leadsheets show a melody written in notation and chord symbols above the melody.

Chords

The chord symbols will always be written above the staff.

Melody

The melody is written on the staff.

Lyrics

Lyrics show the words of a song (if there are any) and how those words line up with the melody and chords.

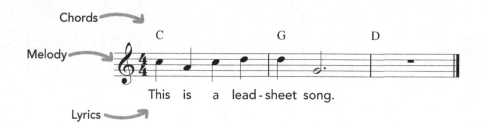

How to Play Your Favorite Songs: Leadsheets

To get the songs you want to play to actually "sound like the song" you need to play the melody and chords at the same time. To do this follow a 3-step process.

> **1.** Play the right hand only until you and perform the melody consistently.
>
> **2.** Review the melody daily as you play the chords with your left hand.
>
> **3.** Play both at the same time!

With this process you can play lead sheets for yourself, friends, and fmaily members and get a "OH! I know that song!" reaction. This way you can take any lead sheet and bring it life...and play your favorite songs in a consistent and reliable way. This is the payoff of your hard work up to this point.

Enjoy this.

You now have tremendous power. You can instantly change your mood and other people's moods too.

Take what you learn and make music to make yourself feel good and to make others feel good too.

How to Read and Play Level 1: Leadsheet Songs: Melody

Right Hand Melody

When people write the melody for a song, they are not thinking about how the piano player will or will not able to use certain finger orders or positions. To play leadsheet melodies, you will need to think outside of the box, position, and finger order. Each new melody you play may need different finger orders or positions. To play leadsheet melodies you will

1. Make your own finger orders and write them above the staff on your music for paper and "mark up" digital music.

2. Look for areas that fit in a position to stay in for a few measures at a time.

3. Learn a few more notes in treble clef

For example, the melody for this example can be played easily with the right hand in G position.

This   is   a   lead - sheet   song.

Right Hand Cross

To play melodies that change position you will cross under with the 1st finger for playing from low to high, cross over with the 3rd or 4th finger for high to low. Use the RH cross to play the notes in example 139 with the finger order below.

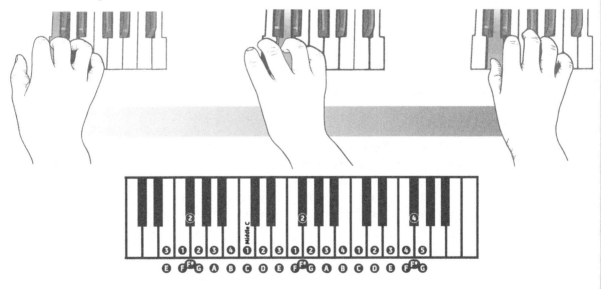

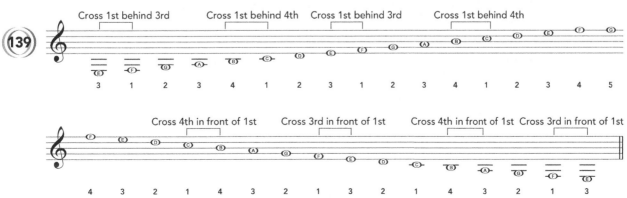

Play a Song Walk-through 1

Amazing Grace Right Hand

Play the melody of Amazing Grace with your right hand only. With pencil, write the fingers you will use to play each note under the staff. If you are reading on a kindle or computer, you may wish to download and print the bonus 10 songs pack (find out how to to this on page 7). Is there a position that will work for the whole melody? If not, is there a position that works for most of the song? If yes, how will you move in and out of that position?

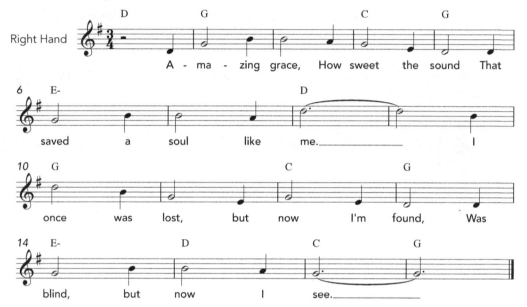

How to Read and Play Level 1: Leadsheet Songs: Chords\

Chord Symbols

Whenever you see or play a C, D, E, F, G etc. if there is no notation after the letter, it is assumed to be a major chord. The same goes for writing and verbal communication. If someone asks you to play a "C chord," it is assumed you will play a C major chord. Minor chords are written with a minus sign after the letter to show that they are minor. Play an E- if specifically asked to play an E minor. Examples of other ways to write minor chords: Emin or Em. E- is the most common way of writing an E minor chord.

Left Hand Chords

Play each chord 1 time in each measure. Memorize these chords and their chord symbols—you will be able to play thousands of songs with just these eight chords!

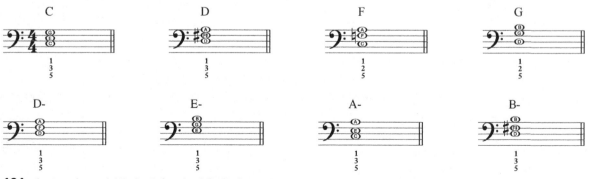

Amazing Grace Left Hand

Now, look at the lead sheet chods and play them as dotted half notes. In lead sheets, the chords are not written out, you only see the chord symbol above the staff. To show you how to think about lead sheet chord symbols, find the chords written bleow. Each chord is played once per measure. Play the chords of Amazing Grace with your left hand only.

Review the melody 1 time before and after practicing these chords so you don't forget it!

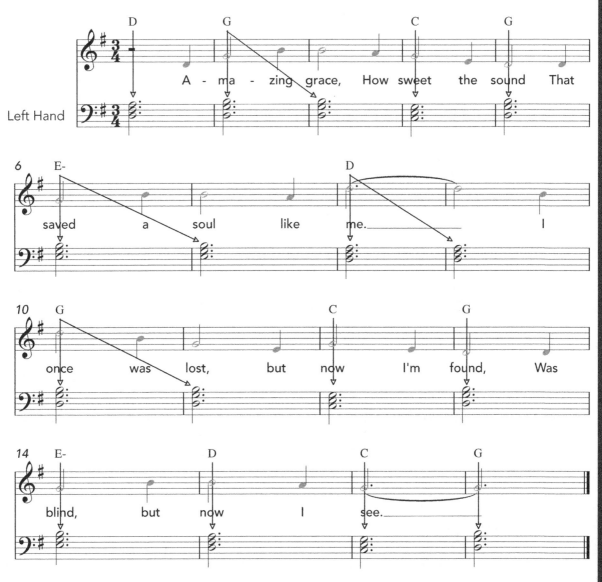

Now, remember those chords as we move on to the next step...

Amazing Grace: The Whole Thing

Now, look at the lead sheet and play it with left and right hand together at the same time. You may need to "chunk it" by going 1 measure at a time. For more on chunking see the book *The 14 Unshakable Laws of Learning Music: How to Master Any Instrument and Singing In 5 Minutes a Day...* **or check the bottom of this page for a special offer!**

Amazing Grace

Music: Traditional Hymn
Lyrics: Traditional Hymn
Arrangement by Best Music Coach & Dan Spencer

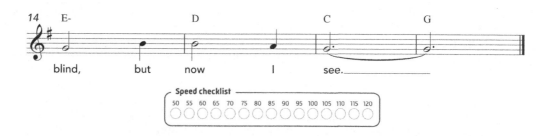

Want 80,000+ songs to play + a free music theory course?
Check out this offer now. Click the link or scan the QR code.
https://music.bestmusiccoach.com/piano-next-steps

Play a Song Walk-through 2

When the Saints Go Marching In Right Hand

Play the melody of When the Saints Go Marching In with your right hand only. With pencil, write the fingers you will use to play each note under the staff. If you are reading on a kindle or computer, you may wish to download and print the bonus 10 songs pack (find out how to to this on page 7). Is there a position that will work for the whole melody? If not, is there a position that works for most of the song? If yes, how will you move in and out of that position?

How to Read and Play Level 1: Leadsheet Songs: Chords

Left Hand Chords

Play each chord 1 time in each measure. If you memorized these chords before, great! You just saved yourself a ton of time. If you haven't yet, memorize these chords and how to play them now.

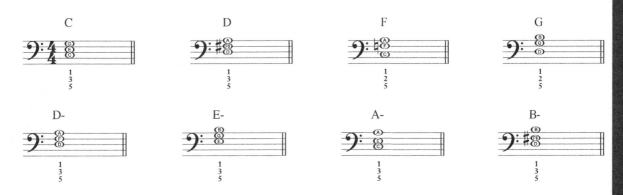

When the Saints Go Marching In Left Hand

Now, look at the lead sheet chods and play them as whole notes. In lead sheets, the chords are not written out, you only see the chord symbol above the staff. To show you how to think about lead sheet chord symbols, find the chords written bleow. Each chord is played once per measure. Play the chords with your left hand only. Review the melody 1 time before and after practicing these chords so you don't forget it!

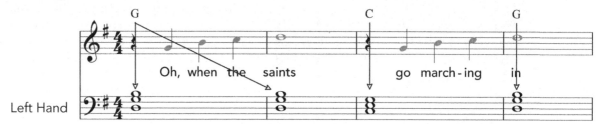

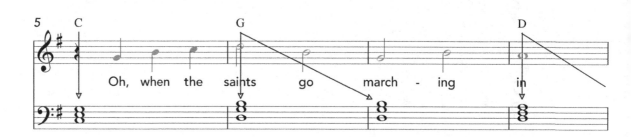

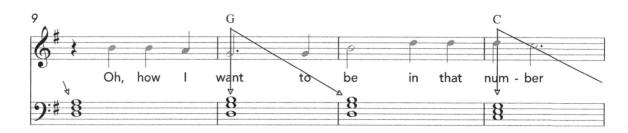

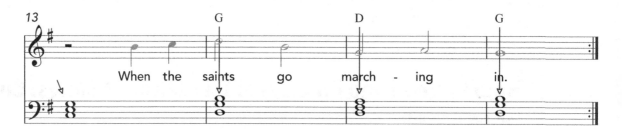

Now play the melody and chords at the same time!

Question: How do I get songs that are this easy to play from my favorite artists and bands?

Answer: All Level 1 Lead Sheet or Level 1 Piano song will be easy for you to play and only use what you have learned in this book. All Level 1 Lead Sheet and Notation songs have hellow badges Level 1 Leadsheet and Level 1 Notation . You can buy songs one at a time at www.bestsheetmusic.com, or you can also get ALL Level 1 Lead Sheet songs, and Level 1 Piano Songs and 80,000+ more songs by signing up for the "Everything You Need" package here: https://music.bestmusiccoach.com/piano-next-steps

How to Play Along with Songs Using Notation or Leadsheets

One of the great joys of learning music is playing along with songs you know and love. You can do this most easily with leadsheets and simple CCM, country, pop, or rock songs. Keep in mind that you need to match the key of the leadsheet with the key of the song, ask your coach for advice on this.

How to Find the Count

Finding where the "1, 2, 3, 4" or "1, 2, 3" count is can be the most tricky part of playing along with songs. The "why" of where the count goes can be understood using music theory, you can learn about this in *The Best Music Theory Book for Beginners 1.*

Count "1"

Along with your coach count just the "1" of each measure of the song. Getting a hang of this and feeling where the "1" should be may take a few weeks.

Full Count

Once you can consistently count on the "1" without your coach through the song, it is time to add in the other numbers. If you need help, ask your coach to demonstrate counting "1, 2, 3, 4" or "1, 2, 3" along with the music and count with them. When you can consistently count all the beats through the song it is time to play! Grab that piano and go for it! If the song is too fast...

How to Get up to Speed

♩=100   means to set your metronome to 100.

♩=60   means set your metronome to 60.

The speed of each song can be different. Look for the tempo marks at the beginning of your leadsheet or notation above the staff on the left-hand side of the page.

If you are unable to play the song at the current speed you can do a combination of two things.

Practice

Use the "Practice Areas" checklist on p. 111 and work out the chord changes or notes that are slowing you down, until they are the same speed or faster than everything else you are playing for the song. Practice the chord changes until you can perform them clean with no mistakes 20 BPM faster than the tempo listed at the beginning of the song.

Slow the Recording Down

There are a lot of software applications that can slow songs down, our preferred option is to go to YouTube and use the playback speed function to slow recordings down, making them easier to play with. Speed the recording up as your practice areas speed up. Keep going until you can play the song at the intended speed or "a tempo." For the best, most awesome, music-making time, practice your chord changes until you can play 20 BPM faster than the indicated speed on the leadsheet or notation. This will make the song easy to play at the actual speed. You can also make songs faster on YouTube!

How to Read and Play Level 1: Leadsheet Songs: With Singing

RH vs. LH

There are several ways you can approach playing the chords for a lead sheet with singing. Since you only see the chord symbol, how you play the chord is up to you!

1. RH plays chords

2. LH plays chords

3. RH + LH play chords together

4. RH plays chords + LH plays "bass notes" or the "root" of the chord.

I recommend starting with **1.** and **2.** then moving to **4.** All examples on the next pages will use **4.**

Bass Notes/Root Notes

Bass notes match of the letter name of the chord. For example, a C chord has a bass note of C. On the piano you can make a very pleasing sound with a triad in the right hand and the root of the triad in the left hand. On the next page are examples of how to play all the chords you have learned so far with RH triad and LH root note. Keep the LH in extended C position, so you don't need to move it around! Memorize this way of playing chords and use these chords for all Level 1: Leadsheet songs!

Major Chords

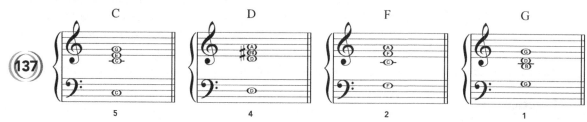

Minor Chords

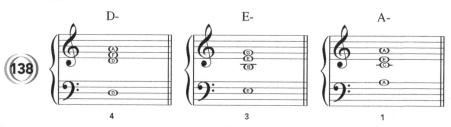

Whole Notes

You can play leadsheets by reading and playing the chords as whole notes. Read the chord symbols and keep the count of "1, 2, 3, 4" going in your head! Play chords over measures where there are rests, the rests show the melody has rests, not the chords.

Rhythm Patterns

A rhythm pattern is a repeated rhythm used for playing chords. Many songs can be played with a single rhythm pattern. Try adding in different ways of playing the chords, with combinations of whole, half, and quarter notes and rests. Once you commit to a rhythm pattern, keep it consistent for the whole song. Some ideas to get you started are below.

How do I get rhythm patterns to sound more like the actual song? Practice the basics first; keeping a consistent pattern through the entire song. Listen to a TON of music to start to hear what different piano players do with different patterns. Then, check out *The Best Piano Book for Beginners 2* **for the next level of rhythm and patterns.**

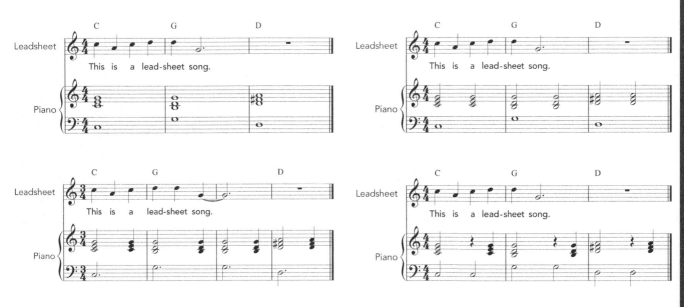

To get more insight into how to sing and play at the same time see *The 14 Unshakable Laws of Learning Music: How to Master Any Instrument and Singing In 5 Minutes a Day…***or check this special offer!**

Want 80,000+ songs to play + a free music theory course? Check out this offer now. Click the link or scan the QR code. https://music.bestmusiccoach.com/piano-next-steps

What is Next?

We recommend that you play through 3-5 Level 1 songs from bestsheetmusic.com before moving on to the next book. It is in your best interests to cement the ideas and techniques from this book firmly into your music before moving forward to more ideas.

Level 2

In the next book "*The Best Piano Book for Beginners 2*" you will learn everything you need to know to play Level 2: Notation, and Level 2: Leadsheet songs. There are many, many, more songs to play at Level 2 than at Level 1, because most songs use a type of note called an "eighth note."

**In the next book, learn everything
to play all the songs in these levels:**

> Level 2: Notation

> Level 2: Leadsheet

We Want to Hear From You!

Let us know what you think about this book, how we can make this book better for you, and what else you would like to see from Best Music Coach!

support@bestmusiccoach.com

www.bestmusiccoach.com

facebook.com/bestmusiccoach

youtube.com/bestmusiccoach

twitter.com/bestmusiccoach

instagram.com/bestmusiccoach

A Note From Dan

Thank you to my business coaches:
Thank you to the people of the DOSB of Delaware: Laura Wisler, Damian DeStefano, and the rest of the amazing team + thank you to the Delaware SBDC: Cindy Small, for helping Best Music Coach and I win the EDGE grant that made this book possible.
Thank you to the people of the great state of Delaware.

Thank you Jasara for your radical support.

If you feel like you have learned anything helpful from this book, please leave a 5-star review to help other people just like you find this book and experience the joy of making music!

Please leave a review

Made in the USA
Las Vegas, NV
16 September 2024

95383529R00077